Pocket
GUIDE
to
WORLD RELIGIONS

WINFRIED CORDUAN

InterVarsity Press
Downers Grove, Illinois

MIN401

InterVarsity Press
P.O. Box 1400, Downers Grove, IL 60515-1426
World Wide Web: www.ivpress.com
E-mail: mail@ivpress.com

InterVarsity Press® *is the book-publishing division of InterVarsity Christian Fellowship/
USA*®, *a student movement active on campus at hundreds of universities, colleges and schools
of nursing in the United States of America, and a member movement of the International
Fellowship of Evangelical Students. For information about local and regional activities,
write Public Relations Dept., InterVarsity Christian Fellowship/USA, 6400 Schroeder Rd.,
P.O. Box 7895, Madison, WI 53707-7895, or visit the IVCF website at <www.intervarsity.org>.*

Design: Cindy Kiple

Images: Monastery: Andrea Booher/Getty Images
        Church: Medio Images/Getty Images
        Mosque: T. O'Keefe/Photolink/Getty Images
        St. Basil's Cathedral: Jon Arnold/Getty Images

ISBN-10: 0-8308-2705-6

ISBN-13: 978-0-8308-2705-3

Printed in the United States of America ∞

Library of Congress Cataloging-in-Publication Data

Corduan, Winfried.
  Pocket guide to world religions/Winfried Corduan.
    p. cm.
  ISBN 0-8308-2705-6 (pbk.: alk. paper)
  1. Religions.   I. Title.
BL80.3.C67 2005
200—dc22

                                                                    2005029025

P   15   14   13   12   11   10   9   8   7   6

Y   16   15   14   13   12

To Beryl J. "Grandma" Anderson

CONTENTS

Acknowledgments

It would be impossible for me to count how many times some-one has asked me for the title of a "short and handy" summary of world religions. I count it a privilege to be able to contribute such a reference tool myself. Obviously there is danger insofar as anything "short and handy" could also become "generalized and false" rather than "precise and accurate." I trust that this little volume will fit into the latter category.

This pocket guide is based on many years of firsthand study of world religions and teaching on the subject at many levels. For a fuller survey, see my *Neighboring Faiths*, and for a book-length discussion of how the world's religions are related to Christianity, see my *A Tapestry of Faiths*. Irving Hexham has produced two helpful reference tools that dovetail with this book: *Concise Dictionary of Religion* and *Pocket Dictionary of New Religious Movements*. All of these books are published by Inter-Varsity Press.

After looking at many sources for the numbers of adherents and the distribution of religions, I decided to follow most close-ly the website Adherents, especially its chart "Major Religions of the World Ranked by Number of Adherents" <http://www.adherents.com/Religions_By_Adherents.html>, because this site takes the ambiguity of these numbers into greater account than do most handbook listings.

Thanks need to go to my friend and editor, Jim Hoover of InterVarsity Press, for suggesting the idea for this book and then letting me experiment with the format. I would like to thank my friends and colleagues at Taylor University for their encouragement, particularly Phil Loy, Mike Harbin and Bill Heth. June, my wife, was with me every step of the way, as always. She proofread my manuscript and had lots of great ideas on how to make the book more useful. Finally, I would like to dedicate this book to my mother-in-law, Beryl Anderson, who is always there for us and who manages to think highly of whatever I do.

1

Introduction

It was New Year's Eve 1999, the birth of the new millennium. A famous TV personality was interviewing the Dalai Lama, head of Tibetan Buddhism. "Would you tell me, Your Holiness," fawned the reporter, "do they celebrate New Year's in the Islamic religion?"

It is, of course, possible that the interviewer thought the Dalai Lama, though a Buddhist himself, was a good source of information about Islam. More likely, this could have been a slip of the tongue. But most probably, the reporter was genuinely confused.

And who wouldn't be these days? There was a time in America when the question "What is your religion?" was intended to elicit an answer such as "Presbyterian," "Catholic," or "Jewish." Everyone seemed to fit into a preconceived pattern of religion. Now we are becoming far more used to the idea that the answer to the question about someone's religion may include Islam, Buddhism, Hinduism or any number of other faiths.

Your coworkers, fellow students or neighbors down the street may be immigrants who have brought their home culture with them. In previous generations, people coming to this country often left their original identity behind them, seeking to blend in and copying the lifestyle of those they perceived as being typically American. Many immigrants even Anglicized their names so as to be less conspicuous, whereas nowadays getting to know your new neighbors may begin with the seemingly insurmountable hurdle of learning to say their names correctly.

Here's the bad news: this book will be of little help to you with learning to pronounce your neighbor's name. But the good news is that this book will help you understand at least one part of your new neighbor's culture: his or her religion. This book is written for those of us who do not know anything about other religions and do not have the option of subjecting ourselves to lengthy and laborious study.

Imagine we find out that the new family who has just moved in across from us is Hindu, and we would like to have them come over to our house for dessert or a meal, but we don't want to embarrass ourselves by not having a clue as to what they believe. Much as we would want to, we cannot afford to take a week off from work to do an in-depth study of Hinduism. We need some quick, practical help—now. Of course, we can go on the Internet and see if we can find what we need courtesy of Google. Unfortunately, although we are bound to get a lot of information instantaneously, we are going to find so many conflicting and obscure claims that, without further help, all of that content may not be of more use than an encyclopedia written in a foreign language. This book is intended to fill this gap.

Everyone has heard certain things about other religions, but few of us are in a position to check out the rumors. Here are some common questions people have:

- What does the red dot on an Indian woman's forehead mean?

- Are Muslims commanded to conquer the world for Islam?

- Do Buddhist monks practice martial arts?

- Is the emperor of Japan still considered a god?

- Do all Jews want to rebuild the temple in Jerusalem?
- Why does the Svetambara sect of the Jain religion recognize different Tirthankaras from the Digambara sect?

Well, okay, the last question is not likely to come up anytime soon in casual conversation. But there *are* many important concerns for which we need to get straight answers lest we embarrass ourselves or, worse yet, offend our neighbors.

What are some things we need to know about a religion? Well, you might start out by saying that it would be good to know what the people believe. Not a bad answer, but—believe it or not—not necessarily the best one. For a lot of people, what they believe is not nearly as important as what they practice. If you asked them to describe their religion, they would probably spend a lot of time telling you all about what they do and not necessarily much about what they believe.

Think about it: two people may hold the same beliefs in their minds and follow different religious practices, or two people could believe different things but do some of the same things. For example, some people may believe similar things about God but pray to him in different styles, or some other people may follow similar patterns in how they pray to God but believe different things about him.

So we would like to know what members of different religions do as well as what they believe. Of course, the doing part contains a lot of aspects: how to worship; how to be born, marry or die; how to relate to people who are not of their religion; how to dress; what to eat and how; what holidays to observe and how; how to make sure nothing evil will befall them . . . You get the picture.

This book addresses these concerns in such a way that you can look up the information you need efficiently. Even though it may become a little artificial at times, we are going to stick to a rigorous set of categories. Each of them will have its unique

icon. Sorry, you can't click on it, but you can use it to quickly
find the information for which you are looking. The categories
are the following:

NAME. Some religions go by more than one name. Sometimes there is a difference between what people like to call
themselves and how others refer to them. At times, believers of a
particular faith may consider what others call them to be offen-
sive. So we need to pay attention to using the correct names.

NUMBERS AND DISTRIBUTION. This is a quick review
of the statistics for each religion. For instance, did you know
that one of the religions with the smallest number of adherents
claims the second largest geographical distribution, just behind
Christianity? Read the chapter on Baha'i to find out more
about this little giant of faiths.

SYMBOLS. Religions usually employ a plethora of symbols,
and many of them overlap from religion to religion, but
most religions also have symbols that are special to them.
Chances are, you know that the cross represents Christianity
and the star of David stands for Judaism. But does Islam have a
similar symbol? Why is there one symbol that is common to
most Eastern religions but that is seldom seen in this country?

HISTORY. Some religions have a single founder whose
teachings brought the religion into existence; others seem
to have just happened. Some have changed a lot over time; others have remained quite constant. For some religions, their history is crucial to understanding them, while for others, the
history of their faith does not seem to matter to their adherents.
It's important to know which is the case in each instance.

SCRIPTURES. Many religions have sacred books. There is,
however, a large amount of diversity in how important the
scriptures of a religion are to an individual believer. We will

give a brief description of the scriptures of each religion and the roles they play in the religion.

MAJOR BELIEFS. A religion usually attempts to help people make sense of their existence. Who and what am I? Why does it matter how I live my life? Where do I go when my life is over? Is there a deity? If so, how should I relate to him or her or it? Does my belief in a spiritual reality have implications for how I treat my fellow human beings? Whenever you see the "thinking man" icon, you will find a summary of the fundamental beliefs of a religion.

SUBGROUPS. "What in the world is a Protestant?" a man asked me recently in India. Good question. For that matter, what in the world is a Shi'ite Muslim? Is the Buddhism of the Dalai Lama different from that portrayed in, say, Jackie Chan movies? When you talk to members of a large religion, they may downplay the subgroups within their faith, perhaps because they consider their own branch the only true or important one or perhaps even because they are embarrassed by fragmentation in their ranks. However, it is important for us to know when some people might be representing their religion as a whole and when they might be speaking for only a small segment of their faith community.

WORSHIP PRACTICES. *Worship* is a general term that may encompass many different kinds of activities, from private devotions to public sacrifices in a temple. We will look at the major worship activities in each religion.

RELIGIOUS BUILDINGS. Most major religions have buildings that are dedicated specifically to religious activities. Most of them (though not all) have offering boxes where you can drop off some money. But that is where the similarity ends. There are many different kinds of religious buildings, and what's more, you can't necessarily tell by a building's size or decorations whether it's crucial to the religion. We will take a quick tour of each kind of house of worship and see how it fits into the religion.

HOME PRACTICES. In some religions, the house of worship is central, whereas in others, what transpires in homes on a daily basis is more important. So it is necessary that we focus on the more personal dimension of how people put their religion into practice in their homes.

CLOTHING. Not every religion requires special clothing, though some do. But even among the ones that do not, there may be specific rules on what not to wear. In some religions, there are particular decorations or styles of clothing that point out distinctions among members of the religion. This book will give some help along that line.

DIET. Food is important in most religions, both in terms of certain mandated meals and in terms of ways in which the consumption of food is restricted—for example, by prohibiting some foods altogether or by declaring special fasts. Needless to say, this is an area in which it is easy to slip up in trying to establish contact with people of other faiths. Most of the time, people prefer to be asked straight out and to provide a clear answer rather than to risk violating a dietary taboo. Nonetheless, sometimes people will assume their dietary rules to be normal ones, and so the issue may never come up until it's too late. Best to be forewarned and forearmed.

CALENDAR. Since one of religion's main functions is to provide order to people's lives, it is a preeminent factor in the ordering of time. Many religions divide the day into particular segments; some observe a week or designate one day a week as special; most keep track of the year in some way and have annual festivals. In today's world, the adherents of a number of religions keep two calendars: the Western, Christian-originated one, according to which this book was published in A.D. 2006, and a second one based on their own religion. It is not true that all religions have some kind of "Christmas," but many have a holiday similar to Christmas.

One more word before we start our tour. Other people love their religion as much as you love yours. They are usually proud of their religious heritage, even if they seem to have little involvement with it. This fact has three implications for us.

First, it means that people as a rule are happy to talk about their religion. If they feel secure with you and do not think you are just setting them up for proselytizing, chances are good that they will tell you all sorts of things about their faith and practices. I have even encountered people who would make up information on the spot, just so they would not disappoint me by not answering a question I might have.

Second, just as you (hopefully) don't ask people about their grandchildren and then, after they have pulled out some photographs, tell them how ugly they are, so you should always treat people's religion with respect. Even if you are convinced that they are wrong, and even if you wish to lead them to your own religion, people should never feel that you are belittling their religion—or them for holding it.

And third, you should not expect people to be experts on their religion. Much of the time, even people who are serious about their religion know just enough to get by. They may be completely unaware of philosophical, let alone controversial, issues connected to their religion. So we always need to be conscious of the fact that when we talk to someone we may not be getting the "official" version of their religion, and we certainly should never push someone into a corner on issues that he or she did not even know existed.

This book will attempt to give a fair description of each religion. Ideally, this task involves staying away both from criticizing the religions as an outsider and from simply rehearsing the rhetoric that may be brought up by adherents on behalf of their religion. Nevertheless, total neutrality is not possible, and there is a good chance that we don't even see where we allow our own preconceptions to color the picture. That is why it is important for my readers to know that I am an evangelical Christian who believes that salvation is found only in Jesus Christ, the Son of God who died for our sins. I like to think that my faith helps me to understand the religions of others more sympathetically, but I also think that it is only fair to the reader to know that I do not believe all religions are equally true.

Having armed ourselves with these thoughts, let us now begin our survey.

2

Baha'i

NAME. The term Baha'i literally means a "follower of Baha," referring to Baha'ullah, the founder of the religion. The Baha'i World Faith is the formal reference to the religion. In the United States, the central organization is the American National Spiritual Assembly of the Baha'i Faith.

NUMBERS AND DISTRIBUTION. Baha'i has more than six million members, a number that, though significant, places it outside the top ten. However, you never have to look far to find a Baha'i, because this religion is distributed all over the world. Baha'i is represented in well over 200 countries in the world, behind only Christianity (in over 250 countries), but far ahead of third-place Islam, which is in about 175 countries. There are still many adherents in Baha'i's country of origin, Iran, but most followers are found all over the rest of the world, particularly in Westernized, industrialized areas.

SYMBOLS. The most distinctive symbol for Baha'i is the nine-pointed star. In Baha'i the number nine is extremely important. Being the highest single integer, nine represents the diversity (the "nineness") that is enmeshed within unity (the "oneness" of the single number). Thereby Baha'i hopes to show that, although there are many ways to God, there is ultimately only one God and one truth. Many Baha'is also display ornate symbols representing artistic variations of the word *glory*.

 HISTORY. Baha'i emerged out of tumultuous times in the Middle East. It began in 1844 in Iran when a pious man declared himself to be a Bab, or "gate," by which God was communicating his message to the people. This man's followers, who called themselves Babis, went one step further and said that he was the long-awaited Islamic Mahdi, the future leader Muslims are waiting for. The Babi movement was immediately squelched by the government, who saw him as a threat to the establishment. Many of its adherents, as well as the Bab himself, were executed.

Out of the ashes of the Babi movement arose the Baha'i movement. In 1863 a young man declared himself to be the rightful successor to the Bab. He called himself Baha'ullah, which means the "Glory of God," and he gathered many of the Bab's former followers around him. The government did not care for him any more than they had for the Bab, and besides, not every former Babi was willing to accept Baha'ullah's leadership. Thus, once again there was strife.

Baha'ullah was not executed, only tortured and imprisoned. Eventually he went from Persian confinement into Turkish custody, where he wound up spending many years under arrest in Acre (located in present-day Israel, just north of Haifa). He died in 1892 without ever being released.

Baha'ullah's life of incarceration was not unproductive. He was able to manage his family as well as lead the ever-growing community of his followers. During this time, he produced a number of books, which are considered sacred scripture by the Baha'i faith.

After Baha'ullah's death, his son, who had grown up with him in prison, took over the leadership of the Baha'i flock. He took on the name Abdul Baha, "Servant of the Glory." Since

Abdul Baha received an official release from prison, he was able to travel in promoting the Baha'i faith, and he did so, including making a visit to the United States. Abdul Baha, though not considered on the same plane as Baha'ullah, held the official post of sole interpreter of Baha'ullah's teachings.

Before Abdul Baha died in 1921, he appointed his grandson Shoghi Effendi as his successor. Shoghi Effendi had a global vision for the Baha'i faith. He established a representational system of government and emphasized the publication of Baha'i scriptures. He is responsible for the authorized translation of most of Baha'ullah's and Abdul Baha's works. Under him, Baha'i became a thoroughly international religion.

Upon Shoghi Effendi's death in 1957, the administration of the faith moved into the hands of the nine-member Universal House of Justice, which is located in Haifa, Israel, and is an international representative parliament. Members of this group are elected by the National Spiritual Assemblies of each country, each of which also consists of nine members. The national bodies, in turn, get their membership from local groups. This system is still in effect.

SCRIPTURES. Baha'is accept the scriptures of all major faiths as holy, inspired writings, and they are encouraged to study them. Nevertheless, Baha'ullah's writings have a special place as the final revelations. Most of his works were originally in Arabic, and they are considered to be distinctive for their straightforward, elegant style. His major writings include the following:

- *The Seven Valleys*
- *The Four Valleys*
- *The Hidden Words*
- *The Book of Certitude (Kitab-i-Iqan)*
- *The Most Holy Book (Kitab-i-Aqdas)*
- *Tablets of Baha'ullah*

These works, as well as those of Abdul Baha and Shoghi Effendi, are available from Baha'i sources at low cost.

MAJOR BELIEFS. Baha'i beliefs center on the idea that Baha'ullah was the last of nine Great Manifestations. Even though we are most likely to see the side of Baha'i that is devoted to social programs, we should not underestimate the underlying personal commitment to Baha'ullah as divine prophet.

According to Baha'i teaching, there were nine Great Manifestations of God: Abraham, Krishna, Moses, Zoroaster, Buddha, Jesus, Muhammad, the Bab and Baha'ullah. Each of these prophets taught God's revelation for his age. This revelation is the same at its core, but it expanded with each successive manifestation.

The most important beliefs of Baha'i are expressed in a vision for humanity. Even though they can be arranged and numbered differently, a convenient way of stating them is in a list of ten principles.

1. The oneness of humankind
2. The independent investigation of truth
3. The common foundation of all religions
4. The essential harmony between science and religion
5. The equality of men and women
6. The elimination of prejudices of all kinds
7. Universal compulsory education
8. A spiritual solution to economic problems
9. A universal auxiliary language
10. Universal peace upheld by a world government

In short, Baha'is believe that under the spiritual guidance of Baha'ullah's teachings, the world can achieve a utopian state.

SUBGROUPS. There are no significant subgroups within Baha'i. This is not to say that there has been no dissension during the history of Baha'i. Beginning with the time of the Bab himself, at every point of transition in leadership there was some opposition, sometimes acrimonious. Although vestiges of those splinter groups have survived, they are negligible in presence and influence. If you meet a Baha'i, you do not have to worry about what "denomination" he or she might belong to.

WORSHIP PRACTICES. Even though Baha'i has some well-known temples, these are not essential for the religion. Baha'is had worshiped for about a hundred years before the first temple was opened. Communal worship usually takes place within members' homes or rented facilities on the first day of each of the nineteen months of the Baha'i calendar. These are referred to as *feast days*. There is no professional clergy. A typical American Baha'i service might take about two hours, in which the first hour is given over to scripture reading, prayer and meditation, while the second hour is a time for planning activities and strategies. This is followed by a meal or refreshments. Baha'i folks are usually deeply involved in local social action movements, such as minority rights and antipoverty causes.

RELIGIOUS BUILDINGS. Even people who know nothing else about Baha'i often know about their large and beautiful temples, more properly known as "houses of worship." As mentioned above, these buildings are not essential to the religion. But they do serve as gathering places for large groups to worship and for special occasions, such as weddings. More than anything else, they function as a testimony to the faith, as community centers and as focal points to pass the message of Baha'ullah to the rest of the world.

The initial goal of Baha'i was to have a house of worship on every inhabited continent (not Antarctica). This has been accomplished. The next step is to have nine temples, eventually to be followed by many more. The present locations of these buildings are the following: Apia, western Samoa; Delhi, India;

Frankfurt, Germany; Kampala, Uganda; Panama City, Panama; Sydney, Australia; and Wilmette, Illinois (just outside Chicago). The building project received a setback in 1962 when an earthquake wrecked a temple in Ashkhabad, Turkmenistan, and it had to be demolished. Work on the houses of worship often proceeds slowly because Baha'i does not allow contributions from people outside the faith.

Baha'i temples are wonders of architectural beauty, usually with an imposing dome. Particularly outstanding is the house of worship in Delhi, India, which has the shape of a lotus blossom, set in an arrangement of shallow pools of water. One feature shared by all Baha'i temples is that they have nine sides, incorporating the familiar theme of diversity-in-unity. They may also have a door on each side, though it is not necessarily functional. On the inside, the main hall is quite plain. It is basically an open hall with chairs so that people can come in and sit and meditate. The walls and ceiling have inscriptions and carvings, but not intrusively so.

When you enter a Baha'i temple, be prepared to observe complete silence so as not to disturb anyone's devotions. You will not be permitted to take pictures, not because of any holy objects, but because it is considered disruptive. Whether you need to remove your shoes depends on the local custom, not on the religion per se. For example, in Delhi you must take your shoes off, whereas in Chicago you are allowed to leave them on.

HOME PRACTICES. The family is extremely important for Baha'i, and a proper Baha'i home is focused on the faith. Baha'i teaches chastity before marriage, and marriage is supposed to be the opportunity for both partners to help each other with their spiritual development. Each member of Baha'i is expected to read holy scriptures each day and spend time in prayer. Children are encouraged to find the truth on their own, though obviously being raised in a Baha'i home gives them access to Baha'ullah's teachings.

Since presently Baha'i membership consists to a large extent of converts out of other religions, a Baha'i family usually needs to learn how to relate to relatives who are still in their previous religion. For example, Baha'is who have converted out of Christianity need to decide whether to celebrate Christmas or at least whether to participate in Christmas celebrations involving the extended family. Since Baha'i recognizes Jesus as one of the Great Manifestations, there is no reason for Baha'is not to participate in Christmas, but Baha'i also has its own feasts, and as one Baha'i man put it to me, "Nobody can celebrate all the holidays of all religions." Not and keep a job.

 CLOTHING. Other than a basic expectation of modesty, Baha'i has no particular requirements for dress.

DIET. Baha'i members may not partake of alcohol or illegal drugs. Otherwise, there are no dietary restrictions. For example, despite its initial origin within Islam, Baha'i does not have a prohibition against pork.

CALENDAR. Baha'i has its own complex calendar. Fortunately, it is essentially superimposed on the Western Gregorian calendar, and so, despite the difference in calculations, all the important dates have Gregorian equivalents.

The Baha'i calendar consists of a solar year divided into nineteen months of nineteen days each, adding up to 361 days. This number is, of course, four short of the requisite 365 (five during leap years), so they are added as special days between the eighteenth and nineteenth months. Baha'is observe a seven-day week, with Friday as the sacred day of rest.

The following list represents the holidays that Baha'is observe, beginning with the ones on which one ought to abstain from work:

March 21: New Year's Day

April 21 to May 2: Ridvan, a twelve-day commemoration of Baha'ullah's self-disclosure, of which the first, ninth and twelfth days are treated as actual holidays

May 23: Declaration of the Bab

May 29: Ascension (death) of Baha'ullah

July 9: Martyrdom of the Bab

October 29: Birth of the Bab

November 12: Birth of Baha'ullah

The following are holidays that are observed without taking time off from work:

November 26: Day of the Covenant (honors the birth and life of Abdul Baha)

November 28: Ascension (death) of Abdul Baha

February 26 to March 1: The "extra" days of the calendar. These days are times for family get-togethers, feasting and gift giving.

March 2 to March 20: The Fast. During this time, each able-bodied adult Baha'i (fifteen or older) does not partake of any food or drink between sunrise and sunset. This is supposed to be a special time for prayer and meditation. (Exemptions are freely given to anyone who is not able to carry out this obligation for physical reasons.)

Have you met a Baha'i yet? If you expect to soon, be prepared to talk to someone who most likely has thought deeply about his or her faith and who will speak positively about your own faith but will also challenge you to consider the claims of Baha'ullah.

3

Buddhism

NAME. The name Buddhism comes from the fact that this religion is based on the teachings of the person called the Buddha, which means "Enlightened One." This religion has many different branches, but Buddhism is the only appropriate umbrella term, and the adherents, no matter how divergent in their beliefs, are happy to be known as Buddhists.

NUMBERS AND DISTRIBUTION. Buddhism has about 360 million adherents, placing it fourth, behind Christianity, Islam and Hinduism. No membership number is easy to ascertain, but we need to be particularly careful with any religion involving China for two reasons: first, because this country's communist leadership has had a policy of repressing religious expression; and second, because many Chinese people do not limit themselves to one religion, often combining Buddhism with Confucianism and Daoism.

Buddhism is an Asian religion. It originated in India, is dominant in its more traditional forms in Sri Lanka and much of Southeast Asia (Thailand, Myanmar, Laos and Cambodia) and has taken on various forms in many other Asian countries, most notably Tibet, Korea, China and Japan. Today Buddhism is frequently adapted and adopted by Westerners, though often at the expense of faithfulness to the traditional forms of this religion.

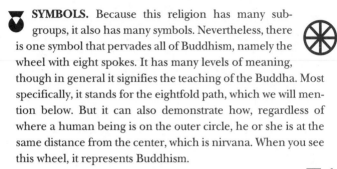

SYMBOLS. Because this religion has many subgroups, it also has many symbols. Nevertheless, there is one symbol that pervades all of Buddhism, namely the wheel with eight spokes. It has many levels of meaning, though in general it signifies the teaching of the Buddha. Most specifically, it stands for the eightfold path, which we will mention below. But it can also demonstrate how, regardless of where a human being is on the outer circle, he or she is at the same distance from the center, which is nirvana. When you see this wheel, it represents Buddhism.

At this point we need to say a word concerning a second important symbol in Buddhism, the swastika. To the Western eye, this symbol is tainted by Hitler's misappropriation of it, and so Asian religions shy away from using it in the West. In Asia, however, it is a common, positive symbol, used not only by Buddhism but also by most other Asian religions, such as Hinduism and Jainism. (And, by the way, the common perception, according to which the Asian swastika points counterclockwise, whereas Hitler reversed it in a clockwise direction, is not true. One can easily find it oriented either way in Asia.)

To the unprepared Westerner, it can be a shock to come to Asia for the first time and see swastikas on religious buildings. However, in its original context, the swastika is not a sign of racism or hate but rather one of spiritual truth and good fortune. In Buddhism the symbol brings together the four noble truths, the eightfold path and, once again, the convergence of all at the center.

HISTORY. *The Buddha.* The story of Buddhism begins like a fairy tale: In the sixth century B.C. there lived a handsome prince who had a beautiful wife and a baby boy. He lived in wealth and luxury, and he distinguished himself by his strong mental power. At his birth it had been prophesied that he would become either a great king or a great monk. His father, the king, did all in his power to raise his son to become an exceptional ruler, but he kept the boy inside the palace, lest he be tempted to become a monk. The young man's name was Siddhartha Gautama.

Overcome with curiosity as to what the world outside the royal court might be like, Siddhartha requested that he be allowed to travel in a chariot around the countryside. The king acquiesced but cleared the proposed route so that his son would not see any old or sick people, funerals or monks where the chariot would pass. However, the gods, who wanted Siddhartha to become a great monk, positioned four visions along the way: an old person, so that the prince could learn that every person will eventually fade and decline; a gravely ill person, so that he could understand the fragility of life; a funeral procession, so that he could confront the fact that all life must come to an end; and a monk in a state of walking meditation, so that he could realize the solution to these problems.

Life of Buddha Summarized

- Birth: Prophecy that he would be a great king or great monk

- Sheltered life of luxury

- Marriage, birth of child

- Age thirty: chariot ride, the four visions

- Renunciation

- Seven years of self-mortification

- Enlightenment

- Formation of the order and teaching

- Around age eighty, passed into nirvana

From this day on, Siddhartha's entire mind was occupied with the inevitability of old age, sickness and death. So a short time after the four visions, Siddhartha kissed his sleeping wife and infant son farewell and, accompanied by a faithful servant, mounted his horse and rode off into the world. Before long, he dismounted, disrobed and sent the servant back to the palace with his clothes and his horse. Then he cut off his long hair and began the life of an impoverished monk in search of answers to the enigma of life. Siddhartha was now thirty years old.

For the next while, Siddhartha wandered around the country, always subjecting his body to the harshest possible treatment, hoping that in this way he would obtain enlightenment. After seven years, however, Siddhartha still had not attained what he was looking for and decided that his efforts were fruitless. He accepted a bowl of rice from a village girl, sat down under a tree and resolved to stay there until either he reached enlightenment or he died on that spot. It was then that Siddhartha found his answer. He became the Buddha, "the Enlightened One." He realized that it was neither in self-indulgence nor in self-denial, but instead in a middle way, that one could find enlightenment.

The Buddha continued to preach this message for another forty years. Many people became his followers, and it is important to note that to become a disciple of the Buddha at this point meant not just signing up for a religion, but becoming a monk. He even included women in his newly founded order. When Siddhartha Gautama died, he provided a final lesson to his community in how to enter nirvana peacefully and meditatively.

Later developments. After the Buddha's death, his religion continued to spread, and as it was expanding, it underwent some major transformations.

As noted above, originally Buddhism was a religion that focused on monks as the only possible candidates for enlightenment. Laypeople could support the monks in their endeavors and earn merit for themselves but could not achieve the final goal. Unsurprisingly, then, within a few centuries of the

Buddha's death, a new movement came to the forefront that introduced sufficient changes to include all adherents, not just full-time monks, in the possibility of enlightenment.

Furthermore, as Buddhism continued to spread it adapted itself in many other new ways, forming numerous smaller schools. Today, Buddhism is found closest to its original form in Sri Lanka, Thailand and Myanmar (Burma). However, in most of the rest of Asia it has found many new and different forms of expression.

SCRIPTURES. Some time after the Buddha's death (possibly several hundred years), his disciples compiled all his teachings into one vast collection called the "Three Baskets," or Tripitaka. They are in Pali, the language that the Buddha may originally have spoken. Their content includes ethical exhortations, philosophical discussions and stories from the Buddha's past lives.

In addition, later on many other writings, called *sutras*, were composed in order to shed further light on the Buddha's message. The best known of these is the Lotus Sutra, which recounts a lengthy discourse given by the Buddha in support of the later, more inclusive, version of Buddhism.

MAJOR BELIEFS. Having arisen in India, Buddhism shares a number of fundamental assumptions with other Indian religions (such as Hinduism and Jainism), though it gives them its own individual twists. Buddhism teaches that each human being is caught in a potentially never-ending cycle of reincarnations. Depending on their actions in previous lives, people will return after death as various forms of living beings, such as another human being or maybe an animal or a spirit. The goal of the religion is to escape from this cycle.

Buddhism's unique teaching is that the way to escape from the cycle of reincarnation is to recognize that the cycle itself is not real. More practically, the Buddha summarized the core of his teaching with the so-called four noble truths:

1. To live is to suffer.

2. Suffering is caused by attachment to this life.	3. The way to end suffering is by ending attachment to this life.

4. We can end attachment to this life by following the noble eightfold path.

The eightfold path, then, establishes the values that can be fully embodied only by a monk (or nun), one who pursues the "right livelihood."

Traditional Buddhism teaches that a monk who observes all the principles and achieves enlightenment will upon death enter the state of nirvana. The term *nirvana* means literally "blowing out" or "extinction"; the point is that the person loses his individual identity and thereby is liberated from the cycle of suffering. Laypersons, in this understanding, will not attain nirvana, but by accumulating merit through a righteous life and good deeds, they will be reborn into more favorable circumstances in their next lifetime.

From early in the history of Buddhism, the idea developed that Gautama was not the only Buddha. Buddhists believe that there were many Buddhas before him and there will be others in the future. Those beings who are almost ready to become Buddhas are called Bodhisattvas.

Noble Eightfold Path

Right Concentration   Right Belief

Right Meditation   Right Intention

Right Effort   Right Speech

Right Livelihood   Right Action

SUBGROUPS. There are numerous subgroups of Buddhism, known as *schools*.

The major division: Theravada and Mahayana. Within a few centuries of the Buddha's death, a significant separation took place among his disciples. There were those who clung to what they considered to be the Buddha's actual teachings, while others, also claiming the Buddha's authority for themselves, stated that the Buddha taught a more inclusive faith in which salvation is not limited to monks. The latter referred to their teaching as Mahayana, which literally means "the big raft (or vehicle)," and they referred derisively to the former (the traditionalists) as Hinayana, or "the little vehicle," though the traditionalists preferred to call themselves Theravada, which means "the tradition of the elders."

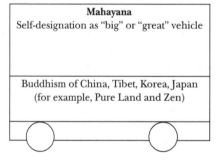

Theravada (belittled as Hinayana, or "little vehicle" by Mahayanists)	Mahayana Self-designation as "big" or "great" vehicle	
Buddhism of Sri Lanka and most of Southeast Asia	Buddhism of China, Tibet, Korea, Japan (for example, Pure Land and Zen)	

Theravada regions. Theravada is the form of Buddhism as it is practiced today in Sri Lanka, Myanmar, Thailand, Laos and Cambodia. Sri Lanka became the main home of Buddhism when it waned in India. There it focuses on the yellow-robed monks who alone are able to achieve enlightenment. There are ornate temples, and it is the obligation of laypeople to support the monks and the temples.

Laypersons work toward a better incarnation by following the rules. These rules that govern the lives of both the Buddhist monks and the laity are called the ten precepts.

THE TEN PRECEPTS		
Apply to Monks and Laity	**Apply to Monks and Laity on Special Days**	**Apply to Monks Only**
1. Do not harm any living being.	6. Do not eat in excess or after noon.	9. Do not sleep on high or wide beds.
2. Do not lie.	7. Do not attend entertainments.	10. Do not touch gold or silver.
3. Do not steal.	8. Do not sleep on high or wide beds.	
4. Do not engage in sexual immorality (celibacy for monks).		
5. Do not consume intoxicating beverages.		

In Thailand, Theravada Buddhism has taken on a number of enrichments. For one thing, the Hindu gods receive special attention in Thai Buddhism, for it was they who helped the Buddha choose the religious life, and it was the god Brahma who encouraged the Buddha to preach his insights. Furthermore, the king of Thailand is considered to be an incarnation of the god Rama.

Mahayana schools. As mentioned above, the Mahayana movement sought to extend the possibility of salvation beyond the monks to the laity. From there it separated into many further schools. We will highlight three important ones.

1. Tibetan Buddhism. Partially because of the worldwide prominence of the Dalai Lama, a lot of people have heard about Tibetan Buddhism. As Buddhism goes, the Tibetan form is one of the most complicated because it is tied in with the ancient spirit-oriented religion of the Tibetan plateau. The essential goal of Tibetan Buddhism, however, is unchanged: to realize enlightenment and enter nirvana.

Like Theravada, Tibetan Buddhism focuses on its monks, called *lamas*. However, it also recognizes a multitude of Buddhas and Bodhisattvas and their consorts. Lamas use different meditation techniques, which include mandalas (spiritual diagrams) and prayer wheels. The common people use the same measures, primarily in order to ward off evil spirits. The Dalai Lama is the highest lama. Whenever he dies, he is reborn as an infant, and officials of the religion search for the child, who is supposed to bear certain distinguishing marks.

2. Pure Land Buddhism. In Japan today, the most popular form of Buddhism is called Pure Land Buddhism (Jodo Shinshu). Here the focus of worship is on a different Buddha, called Amida, who has an all-consuming compassion for human beings, particularly for common people who do not have the ability to put in all the effort necessary to attain nirvana. Amida made it easy on people by creating a paradise (the

> **In the Spotlight:**
> **Tenzin Gyatso, the Dalai Lama**
>
> - 14th Dalai Lama
> - Born in 1935 as Lhamo Thondup
> - Discovered in 1937 and given the name Tenzin Gyatso
> - Became Tibet's political head in 1950
> - Fled Tibet from Chinese takeover in 1959; established government-in-exile
> - Nobel Peace Prize, 1989

"pure land"). Anyone who is willing to accept the gift, no matter how sinful or deficient, will be reborn into the pure land. The paradise is a place of total bliss, and given the favorable circumstances, one can easily attain nirvana from there. Thus, Pure Land Buddhism celebrates the grace of Amida Buddha.

3. Zen. This form of Buddhism is well known in the West, but in Western popular depictions its teaching has often become diluted and caricatured. One is bound to hear any profound or paradoxical statement described as "Zen," and Zen is often promoted as merely a way of getting ahead in one's material goals, such as in business or in sports. Neither one of these adaptations is true to the original intent of this branch of Buddhism. After all, Zen *is* a form of Buddhism, and its ultimate goal is enlightenment, not a basketball championship.

What sets Zen apart is the fact that it construes enlightenment *(satori)* as something that occurs beyond one's rational understanding. Frequently its adherents try to find enlightenment through puzzling over certain conundrums *(koans),* such as "What is the sound of one hand clapping?" or intense meditative practice *(zazen).* The moment of enlightenment is not so much a higher level of spiritual existence as the acceptance of one's life exactly as it is, without further explanation.

Zen is often linked to the martial arts, such as kung fu. There are, in fact, schools of Zen that use the martial arts as a focus of concentration and energy, such as the Chinese Xiaolin school (the basis of the popular *Kung Fu* TV show). However, many schools of Zen, let alone of Buddhism at large, have nothing to do with the martial arts. For that matter, many practitioners of the martial arts, even if they subscribe to some Eastern philosophy, are not adherents of Zen Buddhism.

WORSHIP PRACTICES. Because there are so many variations on Buddhism, worship practices are also variable. Buddhists may insist that they do not worship the Buddha as god, but they certainly give him the highest form of veneration, comparable to that of a god in other religions. The most characteristic practices of Buddhism, cutting across all schools, are meditation and chanting, which bring a person into the proper relationship with reality. In addition, typical religious practices include venerating the Buddhas and

Bodhisattvas as well as caring for temples and monks.

In Thailand it is common for a man to spend some short time as a monk, with the understanding that it is a temporary pursuit. Since Buddhism is the official religion there, the king has important ceremonial duties to perform on behalf of his realm. We already mentioned that Tibetan Buddhism includes rigorous demands to maintain meditative practices. In Pure Land Buddhism, the focus of veneration is the Buddha Amida, and all chanting and other acts of veneration are construed as expressions of gratitude to him. These examples suggest something of the variety within Buddhist worship practices.

RELIGIOUS BUILDINGS. Given the differences among schools of Buddhism, their temples look different from each other.

In a typical Theravada temple, look for the following items. At the front of the temple, you will likely find a statue of the Buddha, usually seated, before which there will be an altar to deposit offerings, such as incense, oil and flowers. There is a good chance that the temple will contain a series of pictures depicting stages in the life of the Buddha. There may be a reverse side to the temple, containing a second statue of the Buddha, this time in a lying-down position, illustrating the Buddha's entrance into nirvana.

The temples of other schools are adapted to their particular function. Thai temples tend to be more decorated; look for a string connecting the Buddha to various other parts of the tem-

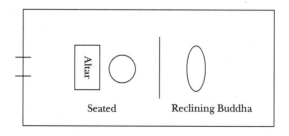

Seated   Reclining Buddha

ple. The Buddha standing on a lotus blossom in the front of a Pure Land temple is called Amida.

The hand positions of a Buddha are important. The three most common ones are these:

- left hand resting on the thigh, right hand pointing downward—the assertion of Buddhahood

- right hand upward with the palm facing the viewer—blessing the people in his presence

- right hand upward with the thumb and forefinger closed—teaching the way to salvation

HOME PRACTICES. In addition to the personal practices to which we have already alluded, Buddhist homes may also contain a statue of the Buddha. Furthermore, even though it is not necessarily connected directly to Buddhism, most Buddhist cultures also put a high value on ancestor veneration, and so a Buddhist home will usually contain some kind of an ancestor shrine. The specific form of it will depend on the culture; for example, Thai spirit houses are different from Chinese ancestor tablets.

CLOTHING. On the whole, there are no specific clothing requirements for Buddhist laypersons. In the more traditional schools, Buddhist monks keep their heads shaved and wear saffron robes. Tibetan Buddhism has various orders of monks who wear differently colored robes.

DIET. It is not obligatory for all Buddhists to be vegetarians, but monks are vegetarian and so are many laypersons in traditional settings. Also, since in South Asian culture it is generally accepted that garlic and onions are aphrodisiacs, some Buddhist monks will abstain from those two spices.

CALENDAR. Because Buddhism is spread over many cultures, different regions have incorporated many holidays unique to them. Still, there are some holidays that are shared across countries, though frequently they are celebrated on different days. The distinction is particularly strong with regard to Japan, which has given a slot to all the Japanese festivals on the Western Gregorian calendar, while other areas assign the holidays on the basis of a lunar calendar.

Here are some of the more important occasions. (Tibet usually follows the Theravada schedule. The Rain Retreat is unique to Theravada.)

Day	Theravada	Mahayana in general (except for Tibet)	Japan
Buddha's Birthday (Vesak)	First full moon (fifteenth day) of the fifth lunar month	Eighth day of the fifth lunar month (Tibet is the same as Theravada)	April 8
Buddha's Enlightenment	Same as his birthday	Eighth day of the twelfth lunar month	December 8
Buddha's Death	Same as his birthday	Eighth day of the second lunar month	February 15
Start of three-month-long Rain Retreat (Vassa)	First full moon of the seventh lunar month		
End of Rain Retreat—giving of new robes (Kathina)	Within one month of the end of the retreat		
Ancestor Veneration Festival	First to the fifteenth day of the eighth lunar month	First to the fifteenth day of the eighth lunar month	June 13 through 15

Buddhism is a religion that combines moral earnestness with deep philosophical speculation.

4

Christianity

NAME. The name Christianity is derived from the fact that the early followers of Jesus of Nazareth were called Christians, which means literally "little Christs." The word *Christ* is based on the Greek word for the Hebrew Messiah, the "anointed one." Although Christians frequently identify with particular subgroups, such as Baptists or Catholics, they also universally claim the name Christian for themselves.

Christianity is often collectively called "the church." This is an ambiguous term insofar as it is also the word used for local congregations and buildings as well as for specific denominations—for example, the Roman Catholic Church. But it is nonetheless appropriate. (Consequently, one should not normally speak of other religions as "churches." For example, do not use an expression such as "the Jewish church.")

NUMBERS AND DISTRIBUTION. With approximately two billion adherents, Christianity is by far the religion with the most members. As in the case of all religions, though, this is a rough number, with no allowance made for degrees of commitment or for the many subgroups. Christianity is represented, at least nominally, in virtually all countries of the world. In what follows, we will draw a general picture of Christianity that focuses primarily on those groups that are in continuity with Christian history and tradition.

SYMBOLS. Many symbols are associated with Christianity, and many of the subgroups have their own. Prevalent images include the following:

- a lamb, representing Jesus Christ as a sacrificial lamb

- a dove, which stands for the Holy Spirit

- a fish, based on the Greek word for "fish" *(ichthys),* which is an acronym for *Iesous Christos Theou Yios Soter* ("Jesus Christ, God's Son, Savior")

However, the universal symbol of Christianity is the cross, calling to mind the death of Christ. It can take on many different variations, and in some Christian traditions it may include a figure of Christ hanging on it, in which case it is called a *crucifix.*

HISTORY. Christianity and modern Judaism share a common heritage. The earliest Christians saw themselves as being in complete continuity with their Jewish religion. However, Christianity took on an identity of its own within its first generations, and Judaism evolved in new directions as well (as you can see in the chapter on Judaism).

Life of Jesus Christ. Jesus was born in Bethlehem, in Palestine, about 6 B.C. According to Christian scripture, his mother, Mary, was a virgin who became pregnant miraculously through God's power. Virtually nothing is known about Jesus' life until he was approximately thirty years old; presumably he grew up in Nazareth and plied the trade of a carpenter. Various legends of supposed travels or studies during this time lack historical credibility.

Around the age of thirty, Jesus launched his public ministry, which lasted about three and a half years. He gathered a group of twelve disciples (later known as the *apostles*) and traveled around his country. His teachings emphasized the point that God expects people to serve him and other people out of unreserved love, not out of a legalistic obligation. He claimed to be the Messiah as well as the Son of God, and he gained fame as a miracle worker and exorcist.

Despite Jesus' acceptance by many of the common people, certain elements of the religious establishment were offended by his actions and teachings. They saw him as undermining their own authority and their interpretation of God's law, and they considered his popularity to constitute a risk, potentially inspiring their Roman overlords to take violent measures to suppress the grassroots movement. The authorities arrested Jesus and bound him over for trial as an insurrectionist before Pontius Pilate, the Roman governor. Jesus was crucified, and his friends buried him as soon as his death had been confirmed.

However, the Christian scriptures claim that Jesus did not remain dead. He rose from the dead and spent another forty days showing himself alive to his disciples on various occasions. At the end of this time period, Jesus ascended physically to heaven, and Christians expect him to return physically to earth at the end of the age.

Subsequent developments. During the first seventy years after Christ's death and resurrection, his message spread throughout the Roman Empire. Particularly instrumental in the distribution of the Christian gospel was Paul, who was originally a radical Jewish functionary suppressing Christianity but who became a Christian leader on a par with the original apostles. During this first generation, several important events occurred: the writing of the books that would become the Christian New Testament, the beginnings of the persecution of Christians by the Romans and the official adoption by Christian leaders of a policy that a non-Jew (Gentile) would not have to become a Jew (that is, not become circumcised) before becoming a Christian.

Over the next several hundred years the Christian church found itself engaged in multiple struggles, both externally, as it was coping with continued persecution, and internally, as it sought to establish a clear line of doctrinal correctness. The internal tussle was also motivated by church politics as local leaders (bishops) sought to extend their authority.

The position of the church in the world changed dramatically as the Roman emperor Constantine decreed in 313 that Christianity was to be considered a legal religion. From that point on, the church increasingly became a social institution and eventually a political power in its own right.

As the Roman Empire split into Eastern and Western halves, the church also developed tensions along that line, with the East becoming known as the Orthodox Church and the West as the Catholic Church. Simultaneous with this increasing rift, we find the rise of certain bishoprics to supremacy in their regions. Most prominently, the bishop of Rome claimed to be the successor of the apostle Peter, establishing himself as the head of the entire Western church in fact and of the whole church by right. The partition between East and West continued to grow throughout the Middle Ages and was final by 1054, though efforts at reunification occurred both before and after.

The division of the church into East and West was eventually followed by another major split in the West. The Protestant Reformation, which began in the sixteenth century under Martin Luther and John Calvin, opposed the corruption and questioned some of the theological assumptions that had developed within the church. The Reformers objected most strenuously to the idea that the church as an institution alone had the power to dispense salvation and that it did so exclusively by means of distributing the sacraments (baptism and Communion—the so-called dominical sacraments—but also, in Roman practice, penance, confirmation, marriage, ordination and last rites) in which case salvation depended on how much individuals participated in the activities of the church. Instead, the Reformers argued vehemently that an individual's salvation is contingent on his or her faith in Christ alone, that the ultimate authority for Christians is the Bible alone and that the Christian's life is to be a life of gratitude to God for salvation, not a means of earning it.

Once again, theological ideas became political tools, and new struggles ensued, not just on the intellectual plane, but also as kings and princes used religious membership as tests of loyalty and instruments of authority. In England, for example, as kings and queens alternated in religious affiliation, much of the blood of their subjects, and even some of their own, flowed in the name of the church. On the European continent the Thirty Years' War (1618–1648) pitched Protestant and Catholic princes against each other.

Further developments in world history also brought about changes for the Christian church. European colonization opened the door to widespread missionary movements, and the rise of freedom of religion in European countries made it possible for smaller independent Christian groups to establish themselves. Currently, Christianity is characterized by two important features: first, a global presence reaching into even the smallest corners of the world; and second, division into many different local churches and denominations, which often differ on only minor matters.

SCRIPTURES. With little dispute, virtually all Christian groups recognize the following two groups of writings as scripture: those books that were considered inspired by the Jews at the time of Jesus, which Christians began to call the Old Testament, and those books written by or in behalf of the apostles, which became known as the New Testament. The latter includes the four Gospels, which are records of Christ's ministry. (Note that the word *gospel* does double duty, referring to both the Christian message of salvation and the books about the life of Christ.) The New Testament also contains the following material: a history of the earliest church (Acts); a number of letters, most of them from the apostle Paul; and a vision of the end times, the book of Revelation. The only major dispute concerns a handful of books, called the Apocrypha, which the Roman Catholic and Orthodox churches accept as inspired writings but which Protestants, stating that these books were not a part of the original Jewish collection, reject as scripture.

MAJOR BELIEFS. Christianity emphasizes correct belief. The salvation of individual persons is the central concern, and if you do not believe the correct things concerning Christ and salvation, it will be impossible to have the right kind of faith that brings about salvation. Here are some of the most important items:

1. God. There is a single God, who created the universe. God is distinct from the world but is present and active in it.

2. Trinity. Christians say that the one God exists eternally in three persons: Father, Son and Holy Spirit. These three persons constitute only one nature (*what* the Godhead is), but this one nature has three distinct persons (*who* they are). There are neither three Gods nor three beings, but neither is there just one person. Protestants, Roman Catholics and Orthodox differ in how they understand the Trinity in certain details but not in regard to this basic structure.

3. Sin and redemption. Human beings have violated God's standard for the world he created. For Protestants this means that human beings exist in a state of alienation from God; their sinful actions are evidence of the lack of a proper relationship to God, and sin can be eliminated by God's grace alone. In Roman Catholic theology, the fundamental picture is the same, but there are two stages in redemption: a person's basic state of sinfulness ("original sin") can be restored in baptism, but to achieve full salvation, the person needs to rely on God's grace to change his or her actions as well. For Orthodoxy, sin is a reality insofar as sin has brought mortality into the world, which in turn leads people to commit further acts of sin, but there is no concept of original sin. Thus, the Eastern Orthodox solution is for human beings to overcome their mortality by participating in God's own nature, a concept called *theosis*.

4. Christ. Jesus Christ is God, the second person of the Trinity. He joined his divine nature to a human nature (the incarnation) and lived on earth in order to accomplish his ministry. For all divisions of Christianity, the teachings of Christ and his works, death and resurrection are inseparable. Eastern Christians emphasize the incarnation, while Western theologians stress Christ's death and resurrection.

5. Atonement. Jesus' death was not just a martyr's death, and he did not just die as an example of God's love, but with his death he overcame the chasm between God and human beings brought about by human sin. In the most common Protestant understanding of this event, Jesus took the punishment of death that all human beings deserve on behalf of everyone who believes in him. Roman Catholics believe that with his death Christ gave us the ability to live in conformity with God's will. For the Eastern Orthodox, Christ's death and resurrection completed the process in which God bestows his divine nature on us.

6. Faith. In Christianity, faith is not just an intellectual assent to the truth of various beliefs, but it is also an attitude of trust or reliance on Christ and what he has done to bring about the possibility of salvation. All major areas of Christianity agree that faith excludes earning salvation by good works alone, but they differ in how they interpret this idea. For Protestants, faith is really nothing more than this reliance on God, and all works are an expression of gratitude or acceptance. In traditional Roman Catholic theology, faith is mediated through the sacraments and will inevitably lead to works of repentance. For Orthodoxy, having faith is not so much something that a person does as a total outlook on leading a Christian life in the light of God's grace.

7. Future. Traditionally, Christianity has taught that Christ will return to earth in a physical body and that he will preside over a final judgment of all human beings. Those who have believed in him will enter heaven, a state of eternal bliss, and those who have rejected him will spend eternity in the torment of hell.

SUBGROUPS. Although Christianity is divided into many subgroups and sub-subgroups, in many cases the splits have occurred over what to outsiders would appear as minor doctrinal issues. The truth is that differences in practice are often minimal. Even an expert, if led blindfolded into a Protestant worship service in the United States on a Sunday morning, might have a hard time figuring out with which denomination the congregation is affiliated. The most important subgroups are as follows:

The Roman Catholic Church, headed by the Pope, has spread around the world, constituting the largest single Christian subgroup. During the colonial era, Catholicism found a home particularly in Latin America. It is sacramental in that it holds that God's grace is conveyed through certain rituals, and it has not feared adapting its practices to local cultures.

The Eastern Orthodox Church is at home primarily in Greece, eastern Europe (for example, Russia) and the Middle East. It is also sacramental and it preserves many ancient traditions. At the head of the Orthodox Church is the Patriarch.

Protestant churches share an emphasis on an individual's salvation by God's grace through faith in Christ alone, but beyond that, they fill a wide spectrum in beliefs and practices. Some embrace rigid worship forms, while others reject virtually all forms. Some believe that the sacraments are ways in which God conveys his grace, while others say that these acts are only ordinances that function as outward signs of inward reality. Protestant denominations also tend to divide over the question of church governance, namely whether a local church is subject to policies by an external authority or whether it is autonomous in its decisions.

WORSHIP PRACTICES. On the whole, no matter how different Christian churches may be from each other, there tends to be a strong pattern of similarity in the fundamental way in which worship is conducted. There will almost always be singing, reading of scripture, prayer and preaching. How these elements are combined, though, does differ. Some groups follow formal written patterns, often called a *liturgy*, while others prefer informal services in which prayers and remarks are more spontaneous and unscripted.

A major cause for division among Christian groups is how they view baptism and Communion.

Baptism is the Christian initiation ceremony. In many groups it is performed on infants and in those cases the usual act is to sprinkle a little water on the child's head, while the par-

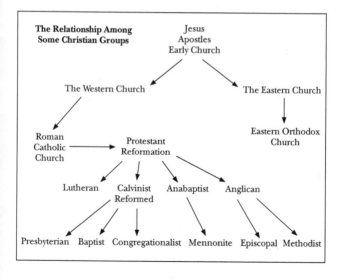

The Relationship Among Some Christian Groups

Jesus
Apostles
Early Church

The Western Church

The Eastern Church

Roman Catholic Church → Protestant Reformation

Eastern Orthodox Church

Lutheran   Calvinist Reformed   Anabaptist   Anglican

Presbyterian Baptist Congregationalist Mennonite Episcopal Methodist

ents pledge to bring up the child in the Christian faith. In other groups, baptism is performed only on older children and adults who have confessed their personal faith, and then it often consists of immersing the entire person in water.

Communion is a ceremonial meal of a portion of bread and a sip of wine. In some groups, a participant kneels at the altar in order to receive these elements directly from a priest, while in others bread and wine are passed around the congregation, who remain in their seats.

But even more important than the physical methods used in baptism and Communion is the meaning given to these rites by different Christians. Even their collective name, *sacraments* or *ordinances*, already gives away an understanding. In sacramental churches, baptism and Communion are thought to be means of conveying God's grace, whereas for nonsacramental churches, the ordinances are simply reminders of what God has done.

RELIGIOUS BUILDINGS. Christian buildings are usually called *churches*. They are primarily places for congregational worship, which is traditionally held on Sunday mornings, though many groups also add other services. The most important room in the church is the sanctuary, which is the gathering place for the congregation, usually a seating area in Western churches. In sacrament-oriented churches, there will be an altar at the front, sometimes as a permanent storage place for Communion bread and wine. You may also see one or two pulpits for Bible reading and preaching, chairs for the ministers and frequently a special seating area for a choir. Some Protestant churches display the offering plates prominently. One would expect all churches to be decorated with a cross or crucifix, and most are, but some Christian groups intentionally do not do so because they believe it could lead to idolatry.

HOME PRACTICES. Christian teaching emphasizes personal devotion and a stable family life, but there are no formal requirements for religious practices within the home.

CLOTHING. Other than a general expectation of modesty, which will largely depend on one's home culture, Christianity has no requirements for special clothing or insignia. In some groups, particularly the more sacramental churches, the priests may wear special robes (vestments) while they perform their duties and possibly also while they are outside their buildings.

DIET. It is an important teaching of Christianity that there is no such thing as unclean food. Still, Christians are supposed to avoid substances that do harm to their bodies, and many Christian groups disparage alcohol and tobacco.

CALENDAR. As Christianity assumed its identity as a religion, it attached a number of observances to the calendar in use by the ancient Romans. In fact, Christians substituted a number of their own holidays for the old pagan ones. The two most important Christian holidays in most Christian areas are Easter and Christmas, and each one has a number of other observances connected to it.

From its Jewish origin, Christianity retained the seven-day week. However, it did not maintain the seventh day of the week as Sabbath; instead, Christians regard the first day of the week (Sunday) as a day of worship and rest because it was on the first day of the week that Christ was resurrected.

The Christian religion focuses on how Christ sacrificed himself for the world. At their best, Christians should display the same attitude of sacrificial giving around the world.

CONNECTED TO EASTER		
Observance	**Occasion**	**Timing**
Easter Sunday	Celebrates the resurrection of Christ	First Sunday after the first full moon of spring; based on the Gregorian calendar in the West, a modified Julian calendar in the East
Good Friday	Commemorates the death of Christ on the cross	Friday before Easter
Maundy Thursday	Commemorates Christ's Last Supper	Thursday before Easter
Lenten Season	Time of fasting and contemplation	Forty days prior to Easter (not counting Sundays) in the West; the period from the Monday seven weeks before Easter until Easter in the East
Ash Wednesday	Repentance	First day of Lent in the West
Ascension Day	Christ's ascension to heaven	Thursday, forty days after Easter
Pentecost (Whitsuntide)	Outpouring of the Holy Spirit on the apostles	Sunday, ten days after ascension day
CONNECTED TO CHRISTMAS		
Observance	**Occasion**	**Timing**
Christmas Day	Birth of Christ	December 25 in the West and many Orthodox churches; January 7 in some Eastern churches (January 6 for Armenian churches)
Christmas Eve	Birth of Christ	Day before Christmas, observed in the evening
Advent Season	Preparation for the birth of Christ	The roughly four weeks encompassed by the four Sundays before Christmas
Epiphany	The coming of the wise men ("three kings") to Jesus	January 6, thus making for the "twelve days of Christmas," in the West; January 19 in the East

5

Confucianism

NAME. This Chinese philosophy of life is named after Confucius, its venerable founder. The Chinese version of his name is actually more like Kungfuze, but it was converted into Confucius by sixteenth-century Jesuit missionaries. Confucianism is traditionally included among the world's religions, though it does not usually exist as a religion by itself. Instead it is a way of life that people practice together with other religions such as Buddhism and Daoism.

NUMBERS AND DISTRIBUTION. Since Confucianism does not usually function as a stand-alone religion, it is not possible to talk about its adherents in the usual sense. Furthermore, Confucian philosophy has not just become a part of Chinese religion but has also integrated itself into other Asian cultures, most prominently in Korea and Japan. A figure such as 250 million might be a close estimate of how many people are practicing a religion of which Confucianism is a part. But if we wanted to extend the number to include nonreligious parts of cultures, it would be much larger.

SYMBOLS. Again, because Confucianism is not a religious organization by itself, one should not look for an official symbol for it. However, when you are viewing Chinese art and you see a drawing of a man with a big beard and a four-cornered hat, chances are that you are looking at a depiction of Confucius.

HISTORY. Confucius lived in China from 551 to 479 B.C. This was a time of great religious and political turmoil in China, and because of his personal circumstances, Confucius had the unenviable opportunity to study the problems of the nation from many different angles.

Coming from a family of minor officials, Confucius studied and edited the Chinese classics, but he was impoverished because of his father's early death. Through hard work and evident wisdom, he was able to raise his status gradually, winding up as adviser to the prince of the province of Lu when he was in his fifties. Despite his own immaculate reputation, however, he fell victim to court intrigue and found himself spending the last thirty or so years of his life without employment. He traveled throughout China, accumulating an ever-growing group of disciples, whom he instructed in his philosophy. By the time he died, he had gained fame as a great teacher whose ideas could potentially restore order to China.

Confucius wrote down much of his own teaching, and his disciples collected them and published them as books, though it would be a few centuries before his ideas would be at the peak of their influence. First, China became unified under the tyrannical Qin dynasty, whose opinions were antithetical to those of Confucius. But then, under the Han dynasty, which came next, the belief system of Confucius became the official philosophy of the Chinese Empire.

In order to understand the increasing importance of Confucianism, we need to keep two aspects distinct: the man and his ideas.

Confucius, the man, became the object of greater and greater veneration, until eventually there were temples erected to Confucius. As odd as it sounds, there is nothing remarkable about this development. From the remotest past, the Chinese people have venerated their ancestors, and the more distinguished a person was in life, the more he has been respected after death. Thus, a man of the stature of Confucius would naturally become venerated by subsequent generations. This side to Confucianism has recently diminished in Chinese culture, but in any case it is not the essence of Confucianism.

The heart of Confucianism lies not in the man but in his ideas and their impact on Chinese culture. His principles became the ideals for structuring Chinese society from top to bottom. Right into the twenty-first century, even though China has undergone numerous changes, including the official repudiation of Confucianism, it has remained the worldview that provides the patterns for community and family life.

SCRIPTURES. Confucianism venerates all the Confucian classics, but it ascribes particular importance to those works that embody the teachings of Confucius himself. Among those, the most important is called the Analects, or Conversations. It is a compilation of what Confucius taught and how he responded to his disciples and challengers in various situations.

MAJOR BELIEFS. Confucianism is about how to create a flourishing society. It does not promote any specific supernatural beliefs, though it does encourage people to fulfill their particular religious obligations as one part of their moral duties. More than anything else, Confucianism provides a blueprint for relationships among human beings.

What is my role in society? Confucius tells me that I do not have a single role but rather that I have many different relationships, each of which entails different roles. For example, I am the son of my parents, but I am also the father of my sons. I am younger than my older brother but older than my younger brother. I am the husband of my wife. As I meet different people throughout the day, some are older than I am and some are younger. Finally, I am subject to various authorities over me (particularly the government), but I also have a certain amount of authority over other people, due to my occupation as teacher. These are, of course, no earth-shaking observations, but Confucianism says that I need to keep in mind each of these distinctions at all times and that my actions should be geared to each of them.

Here are these five relationships, along with the virtues that go with each. The goal for observing the correct virtues and relationships is an ideal society into which all members are fully integrated. There should be no criminals or rebels against the established order, because everyone has a stake in society's continuing along its traditional path.

Higher Position	Virtue		Virtue	Lower Position
Father	*Kindness*	←→	*Filial piety*	Son
Older Brother	*Gentleness*	←→	*Humility*	Younger Brother
Husband	*Righteousness*	←→	*Obedience*	Wife
Elder	*Humane consideration*	←→	*Deference*	Junior
Ruler	*Benevolence*	←→	*Loyalty*	Subject

No virtue seems as important in Confucianism as filial piety. We can think of it first as obedience to your parents, but it goes much further than that. Filial piety includes maintaining the honor of your parents at all costs, even if they should act dishonorably.

This virtue carries on beyond the grave, and in some ways it is after death that it becomes most important. When a person dies, it is incumbent upon his or her children, preferably the oldest son, to make sure that all the proper rituals are performed so that the deceased can have a trouble-free afterlife. The survivors must burn a paper house, paper money and other replicas of amenities (nowadays a paper car is often part of the collection) so that all of this wealth can be transferred to the deceased. Furthermore, food must be offered and prayers must be recited, not only at the time of the funeral, but also at regular intervals subsequently. The living must maintain a little shrine to the departed in their home and burn incense on it twice a day.

SUBGROUPS. Since Confucianism is not embodied in a religious organization, it would not make any sense to look for subgroups. Confucian scholars have disagreed with each other over points of interpretation, and there are some regional or cultural differences in the application of Confucian principles, but there are no major schools of Confucianism.

WORSHIP PRACTICES. As stated above, Confucianism is not a religion about gods or salvation or doctrines. Confucius did not think that any gods were terribly important, but he focused on heaven *(tian or t'ien)* as the source of true virtue and endorsed all the traditional obligations associated with ancestor veneration.

RELIGIOUS BUILDINGS. During the Han dynasty, when Confucianism first flourished, many temples were dedicated to Confucius. Eventually, as Daoism developed as a religion with many gods, the direct worship of Confucius became less popular. Still, today it is not uncommon to find a statue of Confucius in a Chinese temple, honoring his special contributions to Chinese thought and culture.

HOME PRACTICES. There's no place like home for practicing Confucianism—even more so than the prince's palace, the marketplace or the school. It is in the home where filial piety, the supreme value of Confucianism, takes root and thrives. And it is here that the hierarchy of relationships, which is mirrored in society at large, becomes ingrained in the lives of the followers of Confucius.

CLOTHING. Confucianism is based on the principle that how persons present themselves outwardly will bring about inward changes for both themselves and society. This principle applies to a person's clothes. What one wears, and how, should accurately reflect a person's standing in society, and in the ideal Confucian society, each person wears clearly recognizable robes and insignia. In the twentieth century, when China repudiated its Confucian heritage, many men declared their modernity by cutting off the traditional hair braid.

DIET. A Chinese man once told me in jest that the Chinese eat everything with legs, except tables and chairs, and everything with wings, except airplanes. I wonder why he left out fish and vegetables. In all seriousness, there is no hindrance in Confucian principles to the omnivorous Chinese fare. However, food plays an important role in Chinese culture in another way, and this function is underscored by Confucianism.

As alluded to above, people are obligated to provide food offerings to the ancestors. In addition to the regular times for doing this on an individual basis, everyone is supposed to give a meal to the departed at Qing-ming, the spring festival. A person presents food to the spirits, who will consume the essence of this food, leaving only the physical component, which is then eaten by the living people. Participation in this meal signifies being a part of the family, which encompasses the living and the departed. Not to eat the Qing-ming feast is considered a serious breach of filial piety.

CALENDAR. Given its orientation toward preserving Chinese tradition, Confucianism is interested in maintaining a traditional calendar, though during some phases of history China has had both a lunar and a solar calendar. Still, it is the lunar calendar that has become most prominently associated with Chinese culture and has given it some of its most recognizable features.

The Chinese calendar begins in what corresponds to the year 2698 B.C. on the Western calendar, the year in which the first Chinese dynasty, the Xia dynasty, was founded, thereby initiating Chinese civilization as such. Thus, our year 2000 was the Chinese year 4698. The year 2006 was the year of the dog, based on the twelve-year cycle, listed below in conjunction with the next years of the Western calendar:

2005	Rooster	2009	Ox	2013	Snake
2006	Dog	2010	Tiger	2014	Horse
2007	Pig	2011	Rabbit	2015	Goat
2008	Rat	2012	Dragon	2016	Monkey

The Chinese lunar New Year usually falls into late January or early February. It is by far the most important holiday of the year, with everyone receiving presents. People get new clothes if they can afford them. Religiously, the highlight occurs when the head of the household informs the kitchen god of the state of the family. The kitchen god will then make his report to the emperor of heaven, and in order to make sure that he will speak favorably of the family, the family will have smeared his lips with honey. (You see how the Confucian ideals of family and hierarchy are evident even in this little ceremony.) Among the gifts that people give to each other are oranges, whose golden color signifies the hope for prosperity in the coming year. In many provinces, young people receive *hong bao*—"lucky money"—in small, bright-red envelopes.

According to Confucian reckoning, everyone turns a year older on New Year's Day. This is particularly fascinating for newborn infants, who are already considered to be one year old (namely in their first year) as soon as they are born. Thus, a child born in early January on the Western calendar is already two years old in late February—by the Confucian calculation. Even though this is confusing to Western ears at first, it makes sense as long as you know the principles involved.

The Confucian ideal of the family also shows up at Qing-ming, the spring festival. As we mentioned above, this festival celebrates the solidarity of the family. Everyone goes to the cemetery to clean the graves and chase away evil spirits, traditionally with firecrackers. The ancestors and the living share a big meal in the expectation of harmony across the natural and supernatural worlds.

Many of the outward forms of Confucianism have been eradicated from Chinese culture, both by the establishment of a communist state and by the influence of Western culture. Nevertheless, attitudes of submission to authority and propriety in relationships continue to provide a framework for Chinese culture. (Be sure to look at the chapter on Daoism for another large component of the Chinese worldview.)

6

Daoism

NAME. Also spelled Taoism. The name is based on the concept of the Dao (Tao), which means "the Way." Thus, Daoism means "following the Way." It is an abstract philosophy as well as a religion with temples, gods and worship practices.

NUMBERS AND DISTRIBUTION. Daoism is usually considered a part of the combined Chinese religion that includes Confucianism and Buddhism. It is impossible to provide a credible number, particularly in the wake of the communist suppression of religion in China in the second half of the twentieth century. As with Confucianism, 250 million adherents is at best a rough guess.

SYMBOLS. The yin and yang sign represents the two fundamental elements of the universe intertwined with each other. They are opposites in every respect, but they should complement, not overpower, each other. The two dots show that there is a little bit of yang inside yin and a little bit of yin inside yang, thus making for perfect balance and harmony.

Yin and yang represent the following attributes:

Yin	Yang
earth	heaven
cold	hot
wet	dry
passive	active
dark	bright
mysterious	clear
feminine	masculine

The concept of yin and yang is a part of all Chinese thought, not just Daoism, but it is in Daoism where it has made its strongest impression. Note that good or evil, sometimes mistakenly associated with one or the other element, are actually synonymous with balance and imbalance. There is evil whenever there is too much yin or yang, and there is good whenever the two are in appropriate harmony.

Having the right amount of balance depends on the object. For example, it is good when the village well is heavy on yin, whereas it is good when yang is dominant in the kitchen fire. A well with too much yang would be dry, and a fire with too much yin would be cold.

HISTORY. Many of the principles of Daoism go back to the earliest prehistory of China. As a philosophical system, it first flourished in the sixth century B.C., but it took many more centuries for it to assume its present form as a religion that worships many gods.

Traditionally, the founder of Daoism is said to have been an old man named Lao-zi, who lived in the sixth century B.C. (making him roughly contemporary with the Buddha and Confucius). I say "an old man" because the story is that Lao-zi was so wise that, in keeping with the Chinese understanding that wisdom and old age go hand in hand, he must have already been very old when he was born.

According to the legend, when Lao-zi was an even older man, he decided to go west (that is, in the direction of India) in search of further wisdom. When he came to the border of China, the gatekeeper recognized him and would not allow him to leave China until he had written down his wisdom for posterity. Lao-zi complied and wrote down his insights in a book called the Daodejing (also spelled Tao-te-ching), which satisfied the gatekeeper, who then let him pass, never to be heard of again.

Lao-zi's wisdom was elaborated by further thinkers over the next few centuries. Initially, Daoism was an abstract view of the world that sought to fix the problems of China by counseling people to refrain from intrusive actions and let the world return to a proper balance on its own. Thus the basic principle of balance among spiritual forces emerged as the lasting contribution of Daoism and as the foundation for a fully developed religion.

As Daoism developed as a religion, it began to recognize an increasing number of gods, who were thought to govern the world in a hierarchy similar to a human government, culminating in the Jade Emperor, who rules the entire universe. What makes Daoism unique among the religions that worship many gods is the idea that the power of the gods becomes available only insofar as there is spiritual harmony among people, ancestors and gods.

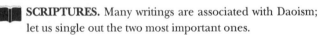 **SCRIPTURES.** Many writings are associated with Daoism; let us single out the two most important ones.

The Daodejing is the book written by Lao-zi at the behest of the border guard. It is not a book about gods, prayer or worship, but rather it is about the universe, language and government. The universe is ultimately encompassed by the Dao, or "Way"—that is, the true balance of yin and yang. If the Dao is left to itself, the entire universe, including its human population, will be healed. Unfortunately, people do not leave the Dao alone but instead try to make a better world by performing all kinds of well-meant actions, which only backfire, so that the more people do, the more they bring things out of harmony. The key to restoring the universe to its natural, balanced state, then, is to do as little as possible so that the Dao can manifest itself once again. The Daodejing also applies this theory to government, so that (to revise a popular saying) that government is best that governs not at all.

The other famous book most commonly associated with Daoism predates Lao-zi by many centuries and is also considered to be one of the Confucian classics. This is the Yijing (also I-ching), a guide to fortunetelling that typifies the idea that in the ideal world yin and yang are fully balanced. A fortuneteller analyzes a combination of sticks that come in two lengths and thereby uncovers the balance of yin and yang for a particular situation.

MAJOR BELIEFS. The fundamental premise of Daoism is that the Dao (the "Way") is the ultimate state of balance and harmony in the universe. To bring about this state, one must make sure that everything is going well in the spiritual world of gods and ancestors.

Daoism as a religion is usually blended with Buddhism and Confucianism. These are some of its underlying beliefs.

1. There are many gods, arranged in power much like a human bureaucracy. Minor gods will serve a small village or neighborhood. At the highest level are the gods whose domain is the entire world.

2. All beings, including humans, gods, ancestors and nature spirits, are linked in a precarious balance. It is up to the human being to discover when spiritual forces may be out of sync and to remedy the situation (a point that does not quite fit in with the philosophical speculations noted above).

3. Human beings have many tools at their disposal to find out where their spiritual universe may be wobbling and to remedy the situation by restoring their relationship with the gods, ancestors or nature spirits.

SUBGROUPS. Just as with Confucianism, Daoism is not an organization, so it does not make sense to look for subgroups within it. Daoism is a philosophy and a practice that can be applied anywhere, anytime. Having said that, of course, there are local organizations and local variations on how things are done. The reality of different Chinese dialects alone makes it obvious that some rituals vary from, say, Hong Kong to Taiwan to Singapore.

WORSHIP PRACTICES. Perhaps, rather than thinking in terms of Daoist worship practices, it would be best to think of Daoist spiritual harmony practices. Here are some of the practices that are most typical for the Daoist side of Chinese religion.

1. Ancestor veneration. An "ancestor," in this connection, is not necessarily someone who is in one's direct line of descent but rather any departed family member. The welfare of the deceased in the afterlife depends to a great extent on the performance of correct rituals by the surviving family members. Each home contains a little wall shrine on which each day an incense stick is burned and some food may be offered.

2. Fortunetelling. Discerning the status of yin and yang, and basing one's decision on the outcome, is very important in Chinese religion. In fact, it is fair to say that in many cases a person may visit a temple not so much to worship per se as in the hope that the gods will provide a favorable outcome to the fortunetelling process. The idea behind fortunetelling is to get a "read" of the spiritual situation with as little human interference as possible. The most prevalent method is to shake a tumbler of flat sticks so that one stick falls out. The applicability of the stick is confirmed by tossing yin- and yang-shaped wooden blocks. The right stick designates a paper with the proper fortune written on it.

3. Funerals. Funeral rituals are a central concern for Chinese religion. From the Daoist perspective, an unhappy departed person can throw off the spiritual balance of the surviving family, and the resulting misfortune can show up in places that may not even be obviously connected. That is why it is crucial to perform all required rituals punctiliously. A Daoist funeral is essentially a lengthy pantomime set to music, telling the story of the soul taking the long, precarious journey to the afterlife, where it will hopefully set up a blissful existence. Houses, amenities and treasures in paper replica form are burned in order to provide for the soul's material comfort in its otherworldly state.

In the weeks, months and years to come, the living must provide for the deceased. If things should go wrong in one's life, one of the first questions to ask is whether one has offended against the ancestors in some way. It may take a séance, undertaken by professional mediums at a temple, in order to get a clear answer.

4. Worship of the gods. The gods are the spiritual administrators of neighborhoods, villages, regions and the country. As such, it is their obligation to provide for the welfare of the people under their supervision. It is up to the people to worship the gods, hold their festivals, build their temples and live according to their expectations, but it is up to the gods to honor their side of the agreement. If worship of a god or goddess does not seem to result in tangible benefits, the deity may slowly fall into disuse and could even be displaced altogether. When you come right down to it, worship of the gods is always a little bit like a business transaction.

5. Feng-shui. An essential part of living a life in balance with the spiritual forces of the universe is that not only one's actions but also the space in which one performs them should be conducive to spiritual harmony. Thus, it is important to arrange one's living space in such a way as to make sure that evil spirits are kept away and good forces are maximized. As a simple example, it may seem most efficient to have the door to one's house facing the street in full view with a walkway leading straight up to it. But that leaves the house in a vulnerable position. So, according to the principles of feng-shui, the door should be in an inconspicuous location somewhere off to the side, and the walkway should approach it in a curve.

RELIGIOUS BUILDINGS. In the modern world, Chinese temples often combine Buddhism and Daoism. The underlying idea is that it is always best to venerate any spiritual being so as not to run any risk of disrupting spiritual harmony. This attitude is reflected in the way that temples often seem like religious warehouses as much as houses of worship. A Chinese Daoist temple will usually have the following components (how they are arranged is to a large extent a matter of convenience and feng-shui).

1. Statues of the gods and goddesses that are important to the community. An outside visitor to the temple may be surprised at how the temple staff has allowed soot from incense to settle on the statues, but this is not negligent housekeeping; the accumulated soot on the statue is intended to demonstrate that this god or goddess is receiving a lot of worship, so it must be a powerful and effective deity.

2. Statues of guardian spirits. The guardian spirits usually have grim, disturbing faces. The point is that they are supposed to scare off evil spirits.

3. Several large pots to hold incense sticks (joss sticks). There are usually at least two of these, one at the entrance and one close to the front of the main altar.

4. A wall or room with ancestor tablets. Even though the soul of an ancestor has been sent off to the underworld, a part of it remains, indwelling a bookmark-sized tablet, which is placed either in the home or in the temple. People come here to maintain contact with the departed by offering them incense sticks or food.

5. An area where people can engage in fortunetelling, as described above.

6. A table or booth where people can purchase joss sticks and other paper products to burn as well as trade in their fortunetelling sticks for fortunes written on paper.

7. A large oven in which people can burn paper and paper effigies to the spirits. Attached to this oven is usually a big drum that people beat in order to get the attention of the spirits.

HOME PRACTICES. The home must be kept free of risky spiritual influences and function as a center for harmony with the spirits. Since Daoism usually coexists with Confucianism, observance of proper Confucian attitudes is also of great importance for everyone's well-being. In addition, following the demands of feng-shui is essential. Also, many people keep their own statues of gods in their homes. These can be purchased in stores, and they become imbued with spiritual power once they have been taken to the temple, where they undergo a ceremony called "opening of the eyes." A typical home will also contain a statue of the kitchen god, who conveys reports about the nature of the home to the higher gods each New Year's Day. Still, the most important object in a Daoist home is the little wall shrine that contains the ancestor tablet(s), to which incense sticks are burned and where food offerings are made on a daily basis.

CLOTHING. In traditional Chinese culture, clothing is dictated by Confucian principles. Daoism is not a determining factor.

DIET. The Chinese diet is famous for its all-inclusive menu, and other than specific local customs, there are no particular prohibitions. Possibly due to the influence of Buddhism, for the lunar New Year's celebration, in some regions, it is customary to eat fried pork on the previous evening and then stick to a vegetarian meal on the actual day. In some provinces the meal of choice for New Year's is wax duck, which has the consistency one might expect from the name and a somewhat sour taste but is not unpalatable.

It might be worthwhile at this point to mention that "Chinese" food as marketed in the United States is usually an American adaptation of Chinese fare and is possibly quite unfamiliar to a Chinese person coming to the United States for the first time. Fortune cookies are not authentically Chinese at all.

CALENDAR. Daoism follows the Confucian lunar calendar. (See the chapter on Confucianism for an explanation of how the Chinese year is set up and for comments on the lunar New Year and Qing-ming, the spring festival of honoring the dead.)

An additional festival that is more closely tied to the Daoist side of Chinese religion is the Hungry Ghost Festival, set in the seventh month of the lunar year (roughly the month of August on the Western calendar). A "hungry ghost" is a dissatisfied deceased person, someone who perhaps did not receive proper veneration when he died or maybe someone who still holds a grudge about what was done to him during his lifetime. The Chinese believe that during this month the gates of hell are opened and these irritated spirits are allowed to roam around, causing harm to the living and consuming unnatural quantities of food. Thus, this month is given over to appeasing the hungry ghosts. Family members may make up for past neglect; there will be a great feast for the ghosts (in which family members participate) on the fifteenth of the month. City streets may have a fairlike atmosphere, with roadside shrines and free theater performances.

Be sure to read the chapter on Confucianism for other dimensions of Chinese religion.

7

Hinduism

NAME. Hinduism is a word created by Westerners to encompass the dominant religious and social system of India. Traditionally, those we call Hindus refer to their religion as the *dharma*, which means "the way" or "the religion."

NUMBERS AND DISTRIBUTION. There are approximately 900 million Hindus in the world, with just over a million of them in the United States. Obviously, the greatest number of Hindus is located in India. Since Indians have emigrated all over the world, however, there are many Hindu communities around the globe. The total number of Hindus in India is subject to some controversy because it includes up to 300 million "untouchables" *(dalits),* who are officially counted as a part of the Hindu social structure but who are prevented from fully participating in their religion.

SYMBOLS. Symbols play an important role in Hinduism, but if we were to take just one as standing for the entire religion, it would have to be the graphic representation of the sacred syllable Om. Om is a sound that has no literal meaning but that is supposed to represent the totality of the spiritual universe. Just as with Buddhism, the swastika is a prevalent emblem in Hinduism, though it is not usually displayed in the West, so as to forestall possible misunderstandings. In Hinduism, the swastika represents prosperity and good fortune.

 HISTORY. Hinduism began as the religion of a group of people migrating into the Indian subcontinent from Central Asia. These people are called the Aryans, but one should not confuse them with the figments of racist ideologies in the West. When they entered India around 1500 B.C., they worshiped a number of gods with animal sacrifices. The prerogative to perform the rituals belonged to the priests, called Brahmins, who recorded their prayers and sacrificial formulas in books called Vedas.

The religion of the Aryans underwent some drastic changes. One direction of change was an increase in rules and regulations propagated by the Brahmins. The caste system developed, and belief in reincarnation became an integral part of Hinduism. Sometimes this early form of Hinduism is called "the way of works" because it emphasized the rules and rituals demanded by the Brahmins.

Around the sixth century B.C., there was also change in the opposite direction, namely a reaction against the all-pervasive rituals demanded by the priests. While this change led to the formation of the religions of Buddhism and Jainism, it also led to a new understanding of Hinduism. According to this new way of looking at things—"the way of knowledge"—the point of the religion was not to amass as many works as possible but instead to find God deep within oneself. The way of works and the way of knowledge continued to exist side by side and influenced each other.

By the eighth century A.D., a third way of practicing Hinduism came about. We can call it "the way of devotion." The distinctive feature of this form of Hinduism is that a person focuses on one particular god or goddess, and this deity provides for the needs of the person, whether it be salvation or this-worldly needs. The way of devotion blended into the other two ways, and modern Hinduism combines all three, with the third way perhaps in the lead.

Here is some basic terminology to go with the three ways:

Way of Works	Based on sacrifices and rituals	Brahmanism or Vedic Hinduism
Way of Knowledge	Based on finding God within oneself	Vedantic Hinduism
Way of Devotion	Based on a person's relationship with a single deity	Bhakti Hinduism

SCRIPTURES. Hinduism has a large and complex set of writings that are traditionally organized into two main categories. The *shruti* are those that were "heard" from the gods by holy men, called *rishis,* a long time ago and recorded by them.

	Writings	Content
Shruti	Vedas	Four major works, containing hymns and sacrificial formulas
	Brahmanas	Instructions for priests
	Sutras	Instructions for all people
	Law of Manu	Specific instructions for all Hindus
	Upanishads	Philosophical meditations and mystical interpretations of the Vedas
Smriti	Mahabharata	Epic describing the war between two sets of cousins
	Bhagavad Gita	One section of the Mahabharata; a discourse by the god Krishna
	Ramayana	Epic describing the efforts by the god Rama to liberate his wife Sita from an evil demon
	Puranas	Stories concerning the lives and exploits of various gods

These are supposed to be the main scriptures. The *smriti* are supposedly of lesser importance since they are only "received," which is to say, handed down by tradition. In fact, because the smriti for the most part contain stories, they receive the greater amount of attention from most Hindus, whereas knowledge of the shruti tends to be confined to priests and scholars. Many scholars believe that Hindu scriptures were not written down until a few hundred years ago; prior to that they may have been passed down orally from generation to generation.

MAJOR BELIEFS. Although most Hindus agree on certain concepts, Hinduism has no mandatory set of beliefs. So, theoretically at least, one could be considered a good Hindu and not believe any of the following points.

What most Hindus agree on. Most Hindus would agree that life is hard and full of suffering and, what's worse, when you're done with one life of suffering, you're going to have another one and another one and so on. As soon as you're done with one life, you will be reincarnated into the next one. It does not necessarily have to be a human life, either; you could come back as a bird or a worm or an insect. What you come back as is determined by what you did in your previous lives. This is the law of karma: your actions in one life will have automatic reper-cussions in your following lives. What's more, it is virtually impossible to escape that cycle, because even your best deeds may have unintended negative consequences.

Thus Hinduism in all its forms attempts to find a way out of the seemingly never-ending cycle of reincarnations and to break the bondage of karma. Views on how this goal of libera-tion can be achieved vary a great deal, but almost everyone looks to one or more gods to find the solution.

What many Hindus agree on: ritual obligations. Even though Hindus may take drastically different views on many issues, such as which god to worship (if any), a large number of them consider it important to maintain fundamental rules of life, such as those governing domestic life or interpersonal relationships. Hindu culture is woven into the fabric of Hindu society, and most Hindus cling to those ritual obligations, regardless of whatever else they believe (just as a nonreligious American couple may insist on a church wedding).

What many Hindus agree on: Vedantic Hinduism. Many Hindus, under the heritage of the "way of knowledge," say that the most important problem of all human beings is that they have forgotten that they are living in an unreal world. There is only one true reality, which is Brahman, the spiritual being that is ultimately beyond our understanding or descriptive ability. As long as we treat the world of our experience *(maya)* as though it were real, we will remain hung up in this illusory cosmos and continue through the cycle of reincarnations. However, if we come to the point of realizing that deep within ourselves, deeper than our feelings and our thoughts, there is a Self *(atman)* that is identical with Brahman, we are on our way to escaping from the bondage of the world once and for all. This Vedantic Hinduism, which focuses on the identity of Brahman and atman, often is integrated into other Hindu beliefs.

What many Hindus agree on: Bhakti Hinduism. The way of devotion has led many Hindus to commit themselves in a special way to one particular god or goddess and to rely on that deity to provide for all their needs. Among these Hindus, some believe that all the gods are manifestations of the impersonal, ultimate Brahman, while others consider their personal god or goddess to be the supreme being. For the devotee of a specific god, the goal is to do all you can to honor and worship the god in the hopes that this deity will reciprocate with blessings.

It is said that there are 300 million gods in Hinduism, but not all gods are considered to be of equal importance. The traditional three main gods of Hinduism are the following: Brahma, the creator of the universe; Vishnu, the preserver; and

Shiva, the destroyer of the world whenever it has become so corrupt that it needs to be replaced with a new one.

Each of the gods has a female counterpart, his *shakti*, who brings out his power. Brahma's shakti is Sarasvati, the goddess of learning. Vishnu's shakti is Lakshmi, the goddess of fortune. Shiva's shakti is variable, including Parvati, his devoted wife; Durga, the goddess of death; and Kali, the frightening destroyer of evil.

Vishnu is also important because from time to time he incarnates himself in the world in order to restore order. His most prominent past incarnations *(avatars)* include Krishna and Rama.

The table below summarizes some gods and some of the common ways to recognize them in their statues.

Deity	Function	Depiction
Brahma	Creator	Four heads
Sarasvati	Brahma's wife; goddess of learning	Stringed musical instrument
Vishnu	Preserver	Blue color, conch shell, discus, staff
Lakshmi	Vishnu's wife; goddess of fortune	Blue color, conch shell
Shiva	Destroyer	Trident, three horizontal stripes. (a) Lord of the beasts: animal skin, hair piled on his head (b) Lord of the dance: dancing on the head of a snake that forms a circle around him (c) Lingam: a phallic representation
Parvati	Shiva's wife	Depicted alongside Shiva
Durga	Goddess of death	Eight or ten arms, long spear, riding a lion

Deity	Function	Depiction
Kali	Terrifying destroyer of demons	Black, grimaced face, necklace of skulls, riding a tiger
Rama	Avatar of Vishnu; ideal king	Green, large bow
Krishna	Avatar of Vishnu; cowherd	Dark blue or black, flute
Ganesha	Son of Shiva; remover of obstacles	Elephant head
Hanuman	Grand vizier of the monkeys	Green monkey, often alongside Rama

SUBGROUPS. So far we have talked about some of the differences in how Hindus understand their own religion, but when we think about recognizable subgroups, the best place to begin is by looking at which deity a person follows as his or her highest god. Although there is the potential for endless variety, there are three main schools of devotion: those who follow Vishnu as their highest god, those who are devoted to Shiva, and those whose highest deity is a goddess. They are known as Vaishnavites, Shaivites and Shaktites respectively.

Vaishnavites	Shaivites	Shaktites
Devotees of Vishnu or one of his avatars, frequently Krishna or Rama	Devotees of Shiva	Devotees of a goddess, frequently Kali or Durga

Some groups associated with Hinduism have become well known, including practitioners of yoga. Although in the West yoga has become popular as a way of keeping one's body in shape, in its original Hindu setting yoga's goal is the liberation of the spirit from the body. The physical postures (*asana*) and breathing exercises *(pranayama)* are only a small part of the all-encompassing demands of the true yoga lifestyle.

Another important means of grouping within Hinduism is the caste system. Primarily a set of social divisions, it also has a profound impact on the religion and is in fact enjoined by Hindu scriptures. There are four main castes:

Brahmins	Priests
Kshatriyas	Warriors, rulers
Vaishyas	Merchants, landowners
Shudras	Workers

In addition, there are the dalits, or "outcastes," who make up about 15 percent of India's population and who have been excluded from society and religion by the traditional structures. Many movements have attempted to redress the problems of the past, though it is not easy to overcome the mindset of millennia.

 WORSHIP PRACTICES. The central act of worship in Hinduism is service performed for the statues of deities both at home and in the temple. Hindus believe that the god or goddess lives inside the statue so long as it is properly cared for. This means that it has to be washed and clothed regularly and be given proper worship. The worship, called *puja*, need take only a few minutes. In addition to some minimal recitations, the person officiating (a priest or head of household) will wave some sacred objects, such as camphor lights, before the deity. However, a temple puja can also become elaborate. Music may be performed, and on special occasions, a deity may be carried around the temple area or the neighborhood.

 RELIGIOUS BUILDINGS. A Hindu temple is usually a highly decorated building dedicated to one particular deity whose statue occupies a special sanctum. Most larger temples house statues of other deities alongside the main one, depending on the wealth of the temple. However, regardless of who the main deity may be, many larger temples have a statue of the elephant-headed Ganesha, the "remover of obstacles," to the right of the main deity (your left when you face the statues). Every puja will begin by worshiping Ganesha first. Most larger temples set up the main sanctum in such a way that it is possible to walk around it (always clockwise) as an act of worship.

A heads-up concerning terminology: As mentioned above, most Hindus believe that the god lives inside his statue and that they worship the god when they worship the statue. Interestingly, many English-speaking Hindus have no problem referring to the statues as "idols," a term that usually has negative connotations in the West. Nevertheless, it is best to be on the safe side and use the words *statue* or *deity*.

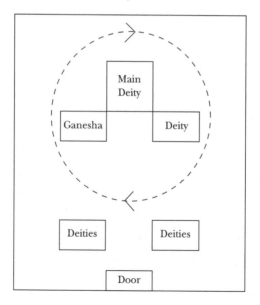

HOME PRACTICES. Home practices are extremely important in Hinduism. A traditional Hindu house contains deities that must receive puja (offerings) every day. In the ancient writings, the roles of family members are strictly delineated. Women have an important responsibility, not only in child raising and housekeeping, but also in participating in pilgrimages and temple devotions on behalf of the family. The traditional practice of *sati*, the self-immolation of a widow on her deceased husband's funeral pyre, though widespread at one time, was never enjoined in Hindu scriptures. Women frequently decorate the area in front of a house's door with *kola* diagrams. These are beautiful designs made of colored rice, intended to be eaten by ants as an offering to gods and spirits.

CLOTHING. Although India is well known for its beautiful clothing sewn out of colorful cloth, particularly the woman's sari, little of traditional Indian dress is considered intrinsically religious. However, marks on the face or the forehead can be of great significance. For one thing, frequently after a person has participated in puja at a temple, some of the crushed flower petals and ashes used in the ceremony are applied to the forehead in disk shape. Many times a devotee of a particular deity will mark his forehead with ashes, using the sign specific for that god. For example, followers of Shiva mark their forehead with three horizontal stripes, while Vaishnavites make two vertical lines that converge on the bridge of the nose.

But, of course, everyone wants to know about the red spot on the forehead of Hindu women. This mark is called the *bindi*, which means "little drop," and even though it can carry multiple connotations in different regions of India, most of the time the bindi tells the world: "I am Hindu, and I am a married woman." When wearing a fancy sari, a Hindu woman may vary the color of the bindi to match her outfit.

But don't unmarried girls already have the bindi on their forehead? Look closely: much of the time the spot is black, not red, and it is intended to protect against the "evil eye." Little children may have three black spots, on the forehead and on the two cheeks, serving the same purpose.

DIET. Because the cow is considered sacred among Hindus, never expect a Hindu to eat beef; it would be a great offense. Not all Hindus are complete vegetarians, but many are, and this would be a safe assumption to make with people you do not know well. In that case, keep in mind that eggs are considered a part of the meat group and so should not be an ingredient in the food you serve to a Hindu guest.

CALENDAR. Hindus observe a lunar calendar, which is adjusted constantly in order to keep it in step with the solar calendar. Festivals usually fall on the full moon, which means the middle of its appointed month. There is an interesting wrinkle to the observance of various holidays in Hinduism. Due to regional and sectarian differences, the same festival is often celebrated in honor of different gods and with different traditions. Here are some of the more important celebrations:

Diwali (late October or early November). This is by far the most important and widespread of Hindu holidays. Comparisons to Christmas are unavoidable because people decorate their houses with lights, hold family get-togethers, exchange presents with family members and send cards to friends. This holiday, which may last up to five days, honors a goddess. Usually this goddess is Lakshmi, the patroness of wealth, but in northern India it is Sita, the wife of Rama (who is an incarnation of Lakshmi). Sometimes Diwali is also considered a New Year's Day.

Pongal (January). This is primarily a South Indian celebration, and in some areas this is considered the beginning of the new year. Not restricted to any one deity, Pongal is a festival of fertility. Women draw elaborate kola diagrams in front of their houses, and men fly kites. In some areas, this is an occasion for adorning cows with garlands.

Taipusam (late January, early February). This is entirely a South Indian holiday. People express their devotion to the god Muruka, the son of Shiva, through acts of austerity and self-immolation. Even though this is not a pleasant holiday, in many ways it has served to bring together the Indian immigrants in Malaysia and Singapore.

Holi (late February, early March). This is a festival honoring the god Krishna, particularly the pranks he used to play on the local milkmaids in his youth, when he used to steal sweet butter from them. Holi is five days of high spirits. On the last day, be sure to wear your oldest clothes when you leave the house, because you may become the victim of a good-natured assault with a bucket of colored water!

We have only just begun! Every deity has his or her own "birthday" or "day of descent." Each time there will be a special day in the deity's honor, with particular customs varying from region to region. Just to mention a handful: Hanuman's birthday is in January, Rama's is in April and Ganesha's and Krishna's are in August.

When encountering Hinduism for the first time, it is possible to become stunned with all the practices, sounds, colors, customs and beliefs. Keep in mind that nobody practices everything but that, for Hindu persons, whatever path within Hinduism they are pursuing is the core of their lives.

8

Islam

NAME. The name Islam literally means "submission," and thus a Muslim is "one who submits to God." This is the self-designation of the religion, and it is always appropriate. You should avoid archaic Western expressions such as "Muhammadanism" and "Mahometism" because to a Muslim these terms imply that they worship Muhammad as God—a notion they heartily reject.

NUMBERS AND DISTRIBUTION. There are about 1.3 billion Muslims in the world today. Of those, between five and seven million live in the United States. Islam is represented all over the globe. Even though we tend to associate it with the Middle East, the largest Muslim populations are in Asia. Indonesia, Malaysia, Pakistan, Bangladesh and India have sizable Muslim populations.

SYMBOLS. The symbol most commonly associated with Islam is the crescent moon, frequently with a star inside it. Though Islam does not officially require the use of this symbol (nor prohibit it), Muslims use it widely to identify their faith. Not only is it usual for a mosque to be adorned with a crescent, but it also appears on the flags of many Muslim states, and Muslim countries frequently have a Red Crescent society, comparable to the Red

Cross in the West. The meaning of the crescent is obscure, and it may not have come into existence until the fifteenth century A.D. The most frequent explanation one hears is that it represents the new moon because many practices of Islam are tied to the lunar calendar.

 HISTORY. According to Islamic tradition, the founder of Islam, Muhammad, was born in Mecca (in present-day Saudi Arabia) in A.D. 570. Mecca was even then a thriving center of pilgrimage, providing numerous temples and statues for the many gods that the people of Arabia worshiped at the time. Muhammad, first as a camel driver and later as a merchant, came into contact with a number of Christians and Jews who caused him to begin to question the religion of his own people. At age forty, while meditating in a cave outside Mecca, he received his first revelation. From then on, God would occasionally pass messages to him, which he declared to the people and which were collected in the book called the Qur'an (also sometimes spelled Koran).

Muhammad preached the straightforward message that there is only one God and that all human beings will be accountable to him at the last judgment. The leaders of Mecca, whose livelihood depended on their idolatrous religion, took offense at Muhammad's teachings, and as the prophet gained greater and greater numbers of adherents, the authorities began to persecute the newly formed Muslim community. Eventually, the followers of Muhammad fled Mecca, and after holding out for a time, so did Muhammad himself. He and a handful of his closest followers went to the city of Medina, where he established himself as the head of the first Islamic community. After his group had become strong enough, he was able to return to Mecca at the head of an army. He purged his hometown of all idolatry and claimed the city for Islam. Once he returned to Medina, Muhammad died.

After Muhammad's death, the young Islamic community

**Life of Muhammad
Summarized**

- Birth: Mecca, A.D. 570
- Orphaned, poor childhood
- Marriage
- Successful merchant
- Age forty: first revelations, A.D. 610
- Preaching in Mecca
- Flight to Medina, A.D. 622
- Establishment of Islamic community
- Return to Mecca, A.D. 631
- Death, A.D. 632

---

split over the question of who would be Muhammad's successor. This is when the two major divisions into Sunnis and Shi'ites originated. At the same time as these internal growing pains, Islam also expanded outward at a rapid rate, so that after about thirty years it claimed almost the entire Middle East and northern Africa and would even establish itself in Spain.

It is impossible to separate the history of Islam from subsequent political history, because Islam is never thought of as simply a religious faith; it always encompasses an entire community, including its government. You have true Islam only when you have a fully Islamic society. Thus, a series of Islamic dynasties provided the governments of successive Islamic empires, culminating in the huge realm of the Ottoman Turks, which was not broken up until the end of World War I. In the meantime Islam had also spread into new domains further east on the Indian subcontinent and into southeast Asia.

SCRIPTURES. According to Islam, there is only one book that contains the true and complete revelation of God, and that is the Qur'an. This book is the compilation of messages that Muhammad declared to the people, and Muslims maintain that its present version in Arabic is identical to the original words of Muhammad. Islam also recognizes that the Law of Moses, the Psalms of David and the Gospels of Jesus are holy books, but since they have been corrupted and their message distorted, they are regarded as not reliable. Furthermore, there are several collections of further words of Muhammad and examples taken from his life, called the Hadith. Even though the Hadith is not the word of Allah in the same way as the Qur'an, it is the authoritative interpretation of the Qur'an and thus holds an important place among Islamic writings.

MAJOR BELIEFS. Certain beliefs are considered essential for Islam. You may find them grouped as either five or six, depending on whether the beliefs about prophets and their books are considered one or two.

1. God. Allah is one God, who can be neither divided nor multiplied. Thus Islam rejects all forms of polytheism as well as the Christian idea of the Trinity.

2. Angels and spirits. There are also inferior spiritual beings, who were created in order to serve human beings and Allah. The angel Gabriel stands out because he is the one who presented Muhammad with his first revelation. Then there are a number of malicious spirits, called *jinn*, who are ready to cause trouble for the unwary believer. The Qur'an tells us that, after Allah had created Adam, he commanded all the spirits to bow down to the human being. They all complied except for one spirit named Iblis, who assumed the role of devil in bringing harm to human beings.

3. Prophets. From time to time, God has designated certain people as prophets in order to declare his standards and the threat of judgment to the world. All previous prophets declared the same message, but Muhammad stands out because he is the "seal of the prophets." He is the last prophet, and in distinction to all his predecessors, his message has been preserved without corruption or alteration. The list of previous prophets includes per-

sons from the Bible, such as Adam, Noah, Abraham and Jesus, as
well as some who are known only from Arabian tradition.

4. Books. Some prophets (Moses, David, Jesus and Muhammad) embodied their message in books. As stated above, Islam
teaches that only the Qur'an is truly reliable. However, since
Jews and Christians also have their books (even if flawed), and
since they also claim to be monotheists, they have a certain
amount of privileged standing for Muhammad as "people of
the book."

5. Judgment. Islam teaches that there will be a last judgment
when all people will receive the rewards for their deeds, either
heaven or hell. On the last day, all of humanity will be assem-
bled before God, and all persons will receive a book that contains a record of their actions during their lifetime. If the angel
puts your book into your left hand, you will know that you are
headed for condemnation, but if your book of deeds is placed
in your right hand, you are about to spend eternity in heaven.
The basis of judgment is whether you submitted to Allah in
your life. You may be deemed to have submitted to Allah even
if you had never heard of Islam but lived according to its precepts, and conversely, simply claiming to be a Muslim does not
guarantee salvation. In fact, Allah's judgment will be harshest
on hypocrites and lapsed Muslims.

6. Decrees. Since Allah is supreme, nothing happens in the
universe unless it has been decreed by him.

SUBGROUPS. The two major divisions among Muslims are
the Sunnis and the Shi'ites. The distinction between them is
primarily historical, going back to the question of who would
be the successor to Muhammad, but there are also a few differences in beliefs and practices. Sunnis were the majority party,
who followed Abu Bakr, one of Muhammad's fathers-in-law.
According to the Sunnis, Muhammad's spiritual gifts died with
him, and the Qur'an is the final authority in all matters. The

Shi'ites, on the other hand, identified with Muhammad's son-in-law Ali, whom they saw as possessing a spiritual endowment directly from the prophet. Sunnis and Shi'ites maintained their own lines of succession, and the Shi'ites believed that their leaders, the imams, had, if not authority on a par with the Qur'an, at least the final authority on how to interpret the Qur'an. Here are some points of comparison between Sunnis and Shi'ites:

Sunnis	Shi'ites
No central spiritual authority	A hierarchy: one imam, a dozen or so ayatollahs, many local mullahs
On the whole, fairly uniform	Split into further major divisions
Mecca as the only major pilgrimage site	Additional significant holy places, such as the tombs of Ali and Hussein
A vague expectation of a future leader, the Mahdi	The belief that an important imam went into concealment hundreds of years ago and continues to live there until he returns as the Mahdi

The overwhelming majority of Muslims in the world today are Sunnis. There are significant groups of Shi'ites in Yemen, Lebanon and Iran. Furthermore, Iraq not only has a majority of Shi'ites but contains most Shi'ite holy sites as well. Nevertheless, Iraq has almost always had a Sunni government, from the Turkish sultan to the Hashemite king to the Baath party of Saddam Hussein.

 WORSHIP PRACTICES. Islam mandates five acts of worship. These are frequently referred to as the "five pillars" of Islam.

1. Confession. Muslims need to recite the confession "There is no God but Allah, and Muhammad is the messenger of Allah."

In the Spotlight:
Jihad (Holy War)

- Sometimes called the "sixth pillar" of Islam

- Literally means "struggle"

- "Greater jihad": the inner struggle of each person to submit to Allah

- "Lesser jihad": the outward struggle to defend the Islamic community

- The Qur'an forbids anyone's conversion by force

- Physical warfare is legitimate in defense against aggression, in order to protect an oppressed Muslim minority or to reclaim what was once Islamic territory

---

2. Prayer. Muslims need to pray five times a day: early in the morning, in the early and late afternoon, at sunset and an hour after sunset. After the official call to prayer, the worshiper has to rinse his or her hands, feet, eyes, ears and mouth three times as a purification ritual. Everyone who prays lines up side by side and silently recites the same passages from the Qur'an while going through the same set of physical postures: standing, bowing, prostrating, kneeling, prostrating, standing. This sequence is repeated from two to five times, depending on the time of day. Men and women pray separately.

3. Fasting. During the month of Ramadan, Muslims refrain from food and drink between sunrise and sunset. This month is intended to be given over to meditation and reflection, and it ends with a joyous celebration.

4. Almsgiving. Muslims are under obligation to provide for the poor and needy, and one of the ways in which they are to accomplish this goal is through an annual contribution called the *zakat*. The zakat comes to about 2.5 percent of one's net gain over a year, but there are many ways in which a person can fulfill this obligation.

5. Pilgrimage. If at all possible, each Muslim should visit Mecca at least once in his or her lifetime. While there, the Muslim will participate in a set of required practices, including walking around the Kaaba (a large cubic structure) seven times and spending an afternoon standing in prayer outside Mecca at the foot of Mount Arafat.

RELIGIOUS BUILDINGS. Islamic houses of worship are called *mosques.* Traditionally, mosques have turrets with balconies from which the muezzin issues the call to prayer, though nowadays this is generally done over a loudspeaker. On the inside, a mosque is usually an empty hall with a carpet on the floor. The only distinctive feature is a niche at the front of the room indicating the direction toward Mecca, which everyone faces at prayer. There may also be a pulpit for the sermon, which is given on Friday afternoon, and some stands with copies of the Qur'an. A prayer hall will either have a partition or a closed-in balcony on which women can pray out of sight of men.

HOME PRACTICES. Since it is not usually practical for everyone to go to the mosque for prayer at each of the designated times, most people say most of their daily prayers at home. This is particularly true for women. According to the Qur'an, a man may have up to four wives, as long he treats each of them equally in all respects.

CLOTHING. Both men and women are expected to observe guidelines for modesty in dress while in public, though the full-face veil, a part of some Islamic cultures, is not actually a Qur'anic requirement for women. Men should keep their arms covered over their elbows and their legs over their knees, while women must cover their entire bodies, except for their faces.

DIET. Muslims observe food requirements called *halal*, which are similar to the Jewish kosher laws. The Muslim diet is best known for its prohibition of pork and any substance that has come in contact with pork.

CALENDAR. The Islamic calendar consists of twelve months, with a length based on the sighting of each new moon, which occurs approximately every twenty-nine and a half days. Muslims do not add any days in order to maintain pace with the solar year, and consequently the Islamic calendar is about eleven days shorter than the Western year. This means that all the major observances will come that much earlier by Western reckoning. The Islamic calendar begins with Muhammad's flight from Mecca to Medina (called the *hijra,* Lat. *hegira*) in A.D. 622, and that year is designated as year 1 A.H. (Anno Hegirae). The year A.D. 2000 roughly coincided with the year 1421 A.H., and Ramadan began in December. Ramadan for 1426 A.H. began in October A.D. 2005.

The two major holidays of Islam occur in conjunction with other observances already mentioned. Ramadan, the month of fasting, ends with Eid-al-Fitr, a day of rejoicing and special meals. Also, during the month of pilgrimage (al-Hajj), there is one day when the pilgrims just outside Mecca sacrifice animals in gratitude to Allah, commemorating Abraham and his son Ishmael. This day, Eid-al-Adha, is also a worldwide observance for Muslims. They gather for meals, express gratitude to God and give alms to the poor.

On the global scene today, there is a lot of hostility between Islam and the Western world. But remember that the Muslims you are most likely to meet are interested in leading a peaceful, prosperous life and are as much appalled by acts of violence as you are.

9

Jainism

NAME. The name Jainism is derived from the Sanskrit word *jina*, which means "conqueror." Thus a Jain is literally a "follower of the conqueror," which refers to the founder of the religion, Mahavira. Even though there are significant differences between the religions, to an outsider Jainism may appear similar to Hinduism.

NUMBERS AND DISTRIBUTION. There are approximately four million Jains in the world today. Jainism is an Indian religion, and most of its adherents live in India. However, strong Jain communities also exist in other parts of the world, such as Kenya, where there has been a sizable Indian immigration. There even is an active Jain temple in Chicago.

SYMBOLS. Jainism is a religion with many symbols, but for millennia it had no universal symbol. It was not until 1975, when a global convention of Jains met to observe the 2,500th anniversary of Mahavira's death, that they agreed on a single symbol to stand for all of Jainism. As might be expected with such group work, the new symbol combined a number of existing ones. There are five elements to this drawing, and they provide a summary of the religion.

  1. The outside form is the shape of a person's torso, the

shape in which Jains imagine the universe to exist.

2. The arc at the top represents the head of the human shape, with the dot symbolizing the residence of those who have attained liberation.

3. The three dots underneath stand for the three Jain principles: right faith, right knowledge and right conduct.

4. The swastika here (as in Buddhism and Hinduism) has many meanings, none of them racist. It reminds people of their entanglement in the cycle of reincarnations, and it also speaks of the four kinds of beings in need of salvation: gods, humans, animals and demons.

5. The hand indicates blessing as well as warning. Inside it is a wheel with twenty-four spokes, one for each of the ancient teachers of the religion (the Tirthankaras), and inside the wheel is an inscription of the word *ahimsa*, which means "nonviolence," the most basic principle of Jainism.

Also, frequently there is a Sanskrit motto inscribed below the drawing, calling on living souls to be servants to each other. Another popular symbol for Jainism is a broom and bowl, depicting the life of the Jain monk, who uses his bowl to beg for food and uses a broom to sweep the path ahead of him when he walks so that he won't accidentally destroy any living beings, such as insects.

 HISTORY. Jainism was founded by a man named Mahavira who lived in the sixth century B.C., roughly contemporary with the Buddha. He was the son of a king who renounced his wealth and life of leisure in order to find enlightenment. During the next twelve years, he lived a life of extreme self-mortification, punishing his body in order to liberate his soul. Finally, after pushing his body to the brink of death many times, he experienced a flash of enlightenment. He received complete peace of mind and a state of omniscience that allowed him to be aware of all truth in the universe and all his previous lives. However (unlike the Buddha's case), this experience did not cause Mahavira to cease his ascetic lifestyle. He continued to live in the same way and recruited followers to emulate his experience.

Jainism broke with Hinduism because it did not acknowledge the caste system or the Hindu scriptures as divine. Furthermore, due to Jainism's central exhortation not to harm any living beings, standard occupations such as farming (which involves killing plants) were closed to its followers. Thus, Jainism began its existence in the role of a minority religion—but this is a role of which it has made the most. Jain laypersons focused on commerce and finance, where they became quite successful, and to this day Jains are most likely associated with that segment of the population.

SCRIPTURES. Jainism produced its share of sacred writings, but it is hard to point to any one book as *the* scripture of Jainism. The two main subgroups each have their own writings. The most popular collection is called the Agam Sutras, but they do not receive universal acceptance by Jains.

MAJOR BELIEFS. Like most South Asian religions, Jainism's main focus is on a person's liberation from the cycle of reincarnation. Again, similarly to Hinduism and Buddhism, this religion teaches the law of karma, namely that our present actions will directly influence what kind of a being we will be in the next life. However, Jainism has its own way of picturing these realities.

Jainism does not teach that we are all part of one massive spiritual reality but rather that each individual living being is a distinct soul with its own identity. This soul, called a *jiva*, is trapped in the cycle of births and rebirths but would, if given a chance, rise to the top of the universe, where it could enjoy peace. What prevents this happy outcome is the presence of *ajiva*, or dead matter, which clings to the soul and keeps it trapped in its current bondage. Jainism pictures this ajiva as physical granules that weigh the soul down, and the more bad karma one accrues, the more ajiva gets piled on one's jiva. Thus the point of the religion is to purify one's soul of all ajiva in order to enter the permanent state of bliss.

Removal of the karma matter from one's soul is something all persons need to do for themselves. Gods play at best an ambivalent role in Jainism. It vigorously denies the existence of a creator or sustainer of the universe. The gods of Hinduism are considered as being real but also as being every bit as much in need of salvation as are human beings. Because of the gods' greater power, a Jain layperson may call on a deity for this-worldly help, but the gods are powerless when it comes to anyone's salvation, even their own. They must wait until they are reborn in human form themselves before they can attain enlightenment.

Ultimately, only those who are able to devote their entire lives to the realization of liberation will attain release. It takes the full energy of a monk or nun to do justice to the five vows necessary to attain this goal.

1. Never harm any living being. This is *ahimsa*, the most basic principle of Jainism, and a fully devoted monk will do all he can do to avoid harming even the smallest insect or plant. Eating is an unavoidable compromise, though in the end a monk will even give up food in order to remove all karma. For laypeople, this vow translates into maintaining a vegetarian diet.

2. Always tell the truth. All truth is relative to a person's point of view and so can easily be misunderstood. Thus one must qualify all of one's speech so that no one can accidentally hear an unintended falsehood.

3. Never steal property.

4. Avoid all sexual contact. Again, laypeople will observe a less stringent version, namely marital fidelity.

5. Do not get attached to anything in the material world. Part

of the idea here is to limit one's sensory input as much as possible. The less one senses, the less one is attached and the more likely one's soul will be freed.

Mahavira showed the way to enlightenment. He was a jina (a "conqueror") and a Tirthankara (a "ford finder"). As a matter of fact, Jainism teaches that he was the last of twenty-four similar Tirthankaras, who appeared in previous ages. The further we go back in time, the taller the Tirthankaras were and the longer they lived, but they all had a similar story as the off-spring of royalty who sought and taught the way to liberation. Even though the Tirthankaras are decidedly not gods, they are worshiped like gods in Jain temples.

SUBGROUPS. There are two major subgroups of Jainism and a number of smaller ones. One group goes by the name of Svetambara, which means "clad in white," referring to the white clothes worn by their monks. The other main sect is the Digambara, meaning "clad in atmosphere," indicating that their monks wear air only.

This sartorial distinction carries some further differentiations. Since the Digambara hold that one cannot attain enlightenment while wearing clothes, and since they say that it would be wrong for a woman ever to go naked, they do not believe that any person can ever be saved while incarnated in a female body. The Svetambara agree that a woman should never be without clothes, but since they do believe that salvation is possible while wearing white cloth, they allow for the liberation of women as well as men. In fact, because of this distinction, the list of Tirthankaras differs between these sects as well, with Svetambaras saying that one of them, named Subidhi, was female.

WORSHIP PRACTICES. For the devoted Jain monk, worship is not a viable concept. He or she finds enlightenment by strictly observing precepts. Reliance on any supernatural agency will only get in the way of one's own efforts. Ideally, the ascetic will bring life to a culmination by fasting in a terminal act of meditation, thus assuring the removal of all remaining karma.

For Jain laypeople, worship is an important way of preparing for future incarnations that hopefully will make liberation possible. In a Jain temple, people focus on the teachings of the Tirthankaras and venerate their statues by waving lights, brushes and mirrors in front of them. Also, worshipers sit at low tables on which there are grains of rice and make designs, such as the swastika symbol, as a focus for their meditation.

RELIGIOUS BUILDINGS. Jain temples are usually highly ornate and, in distinction to Hindu and Buddhist temples, are usually white on the outside. On the inside, there are various aids to meditation, such as decorations and the above-mentioned tables. The statues of Tirthankaras are separated from the main hall, and worshipers may enter that area only if they have covered their faces so as not to contaminate the purity of the area with their breath.

HOME PRACTICES. As pointed out above, Jain belief holds that laypersons can work to reduce their karma, not in order to attain salvation, but so as to improve their chances of enlightenment in the next life. In the meantime, pure Jain doctrine does not provide help for this-worldly problems. Daily reflection on Jain principles is important, but for the common person, so is the observance of whatever spiritual help one may need to make it through life's mundane affairs. So, if you visit a Jain home, do not be surprised to find objects associated with Hindu practice.

CLOTHING. As stated above, the major division among Jains has to do with the clothing—or absence thereof—of the monks. However, laypersons are not directly affected by these rules. They need to dress modestly, but they are not required to wear particular types of clothes.

DIET. How can you eat anything if you are never supposed to harm any living beings and if food, by its nature, is derived from living beings? Laypeople stick strictly to a vegetarian diet, but since plants are also living beings, this is still a compromise, and Jains know that they are incurring karma in the process. Monks attempt to reduce this liability by never eating anything unless it was already designated to be thrown away. But even this measure is not considered to be effective by itself, which is why the monk's life is supposed to end with the act of self-starvation. Since it is unlikely that you will have Jain monks for dinner in your home, you will be perfectly all right in serving a purely vegetarian meal to Jain acquaintances. (This is not to say that a Jain monk might not come to a Jain person's home, but then it would usually be only to observe a fast together.)

CALENDAR. Jains follow a lunar calendar, adjusted to keep step with the solar year. All groups celebrate the birthday of Mahavira, which falls roughly into April by the Gregorian calendar. The second major commemoration is an annual time of fasting, reflection and prayer, which can last up to ten days. During this time, monks and laypeople spend time together in the temple, reaffirming what might otherwise be a tenuous bond between them. But the two main sects follow different schedules; the Svetambaras have their event (which they call Paryushan) in August, while the Digambaras observe their fast (called Das Lakshan) in September.

Because Jainism has produced a culture based on rigorous ethical principles, particularly a high respect for truth, Jain businesspeople have a reputation for meticulous honesty.

10

Judaism

NAME. The name is derived from the tribe of Judah, one of the twelve ancient tribes of Israel. So, literally, it is the religion of those who come from the tribe of Judah, who are (in English) called the Jews. However, a small word of caution is in order. Being Jewish refers to an ethnic identity as well as a faith, and nowadays there are many Jews who do not practice the Jewish faith, even though they are happy to be known as Jews ethnically and culturally.

NUMBERS AND DISTRIBUTION. The ambivalence concerning the name continues in the count of adherents. It is estimated that there are about 14 million Jews in the world today, but many of them do not practice any religion. The Jewish population of the United States numbers about 4.5 million.

SYMBOLS. There's no question about it: the symbol of Judaism is the Star of David, two interlaced triangles. Not that this sign actually has anything to do with Judaism. It might be more appropriate to use the menorah (the seven-branched candlestick) or the two tablets of the Law, since they are actually important parts of the religion, but the Star of David holds the franchise.

HISTORY. Judaism has a number of points in time that could be considered its beginning. Around 2200 B.C., God chose Abraham to become the father of the covenant nation. In the fifteenth century B.C., Moses received the Ten Commandments and the laws of Judaism from God. The first temple was built by Solomon in about 950 B.C., and the second temple was constructed around 540 B.C. All of these are important moments in the history of Judaism. But in a significant way, the contemporary religion of Judaism did not begin until A.D. 70, when the Romans destroyed the temple in Jerusalem and the religion had to find a way to survive apart from the sacrifices and other rituals that had been a part of the temple service.

As Judaism developed its teachings on the inside, it had to fight for its existence on the outside. It was the religion of a people dispersed around the world, whose religion often was their only possession as they were forced to move over and over again. Over the millennia, there were a number of geographic centers where Judaism thrived. For the first few hundred years after the dispersal from Palestine, the Jews were able to flourish in Persia (present-day Iran), and from there a strong Jewish culture developed in Spain. Expelled from Spain by Ferdinand and Isabella in 1492, the Jews' center of settlement was northern and eastern Europe. While seeking to find security either in assimilating to their host countries or in maintaining a self-sufficient culture, they knew that persecution was never far away.

In the nineteenth century, under the leadership of the Austrian journalist Theodor Herzl, the Zionist movement taught that Jews would never be secure unless they were able to occupy a country of their own. As a consequence, many Jews started to emigrate to Palestine, where they prepared to establish a state. When the horrors of the Nazi Holocaust came to the attention of the world, this reality became the impetus for the United Nations to permit the founding of an independent state of Israel. Whether the Zionist vision of security for all Jews on the basis of an independent state is now being fulfilled remains a question.

SCRIPTURES. For Judaism, the most important religious writing is the Torah, the first five books of the Bible, which orthodox Jews believe were revealed by God to Moses on Mount Sinai. The Torah is only one part of the sacred scriptures. The Jewish name for this collection is the Tanakh, an embellishment of the three letters—T, N, K— standing for the three sections of the Jewish Bible: T for Torah (the Law); N for Neviim (the prophets); K for Ketuvim (the writings). These scriptures were already considered sacred while the temple still stood in Jerusalem (and they have also been maintained as sacred by Christians under the name Old Testament).

After the destruction of the temple and the dispersal of the nation, the rabbis started to put down in writing interpretations of the Law that up till then had only been oral. For many centuries the teachers (rabbis) had worked on interpreting the Law of Moses to people far removed in time from its original setting, but only now were those interpretations recorded in writing. First there was the Mishnah, a sizable collection, finished in the third century A.D. But then the Mishnah was incorporated into a far more voluminous compilation called the Talmud, which became the standard set of interpretations for Jewish life. The Talmud was finished by about A.D. 500, and from then on the Talmud became authoritative for orthodox Jews as well as the subject of interpretation by scholars and teachers.

One other set of writings needs to be mentioned. The Judaism of the rabbis has traditionally been accompanied by a mystical form of Judaism, which focuses on the possibility of a person's close relationship to God. This dimension of Judaism, called Kabbalah, has also produced numerous writings, the most famous of which is the book called the Zohar, written in the thirteenth century A.D. by a Spanish Jew named Moses de Leon.

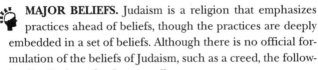 **MAJOR BELIEFS.** Judaism is a religion that emphasizes practices ahead of beliefs, though the practices are deeply embedded in a set of beliefs. Although there is no official formulation of the beliefs of Judaism, such as a creed, the following list displays what Jews usually accept as true.

1. There is only one God.

2. This God has chosen one people—the Jews—to be his special representatives on earth.

3. God's choice of these people is an expression of his love for them, but it is primarily a special call to his people to be obedient to his Law. The Jews are supposed to be God's witnesses to the world that it is possible to live a pure and righteous life.

4. Jews who live up to their calling will receive an eternal reward, but so will Gentiles (non-Jews) who live according to lesser standards than God's expectations of Jews. Thus—and this is a crucial point in understanding Judaism—even though righteous Jews and Gentiles will go to heaven, the main concern of the religion is not to find a way to heaven but simply to live in conformity with divine expectations.

5. At the end of the age, God will send a special person, the Messiah, who will preside over a time of peace and prosperity in the world.

SUBGROUPS. Even though there are a number of minor divisions among Jews, many of which are based on the geographical locations where Jews have lived over the last two thousand years, the major subgroups of Judaism are few and relatively flexible.

Orthodox Judaism involves strict adherence to the Law in all respects. With no further qualifications, to be a Jew theoretically means to be an orthodox Jew, that is to say, someone who observes all the obligations stated in the Law and amplified in the Talmud.

Hasidic Judaism is practiced by orthodox Jews whose heritage goes back to a mystical reformer named Baal Shem Tov in eighteenth-century Poland. He taught that Jews could find God in a personal, joyous experience of his presence, rather than just by following the traditional forms of legalism and ancient culture. Paradoxically, Baal Shem Tov's followers made his new forms obligatory. For example, whereas he taught that Jews were free to wear the long black coats that were fashionable in Poland at the time, his followers kept the long black coats mandatory long after they went out of fashion. Today there are many minor groups of Hasidic Jews, usually identified by the names of the villages in Eastern Europe where they once thrived. After the East European pogroms and the Nazi Holocaust, most of the Hasidic communities that survived were ones that relocated to North America and Israel.

Reform Judaism arose out of a new mindset that was born in Germany in the eighteenth century and found full expression in Germany and the United States in the nineteenth century. This new branch of Judaism focused on the idea that Jews should be at home in whatever country they lived and that the culture of their host country should be their predominant culture as well. Reform Judaism said that the Talmud is not binding on Jews and that Jews should work for the betterment of the present world, not wait for a future messianic kingdom. It adopted European Protestant worship forms in which men and women sit together and follow a liturgy similar to Christian worship. Reform Judaism is popular today in the United States and in Europe. There is also a strong presence of Reform Judaism in Israel, but while the state of Israel recognizes Reform Jews as Jews per se, it does not recognize functions performed by Reform rabbis, such as marriages, as valid.

Conservative Judaism arose in the United States in the 1920s as an attempt to mediate between the Orthodox and Reform sides. Conservative Judaism recognizes the Law as binding but permits adaptation of it in light of modern developments.

Among practicing Jews in the United States today, Conservatives are in the majority, partially because in many towns where it is not feasible to maintain more than one synagogue, a Conservative approach represents a workable compromise.

WORSHIP PRACTICES. Orthodox Jewish worship focuses on God and the fact that he has given his Law to his people. Prayer is a very important aspect of this worship. Jewish men pray three times a day: morning, noon and evening. If a group of ten or more men get together in a synagogue, they can recite a more extended service. Orthodox prayer requires the wearing of phylacteries and a prayer shawl. Phylacteries *(tefillin)* are two little boxes, about one inch cubed, that are strapped to the forehead and the left hand, containing little parchments of scripture verses. The shawl *(tallith)* is rectangular, about two feet by one foot, white with blue stripes and tassels on the ends, which is wrapped over one's shoulder and, at appropriate moments, over the head. The prayers are formalized recitations said in Hebrew.

Jewish congregational worship takes place on the Sabbath, which begins on Friday evening and ends on Saturday evening. The main service is usually on Saturday morning, but some groups emphasize a Friday night worship service as well. The service begins with the lighting of the menorah, the seven-branched candelabra. In addition to a number of prayers of praise and petition, there will be a reading from the Torah. Many synagogues observe a procession in which the Torah is carried around the congregation, with everyone greeting it affectionately as a letter from their beloved heavenly Father. The music of the service is under the direction of the cantor, a person whose training is as rigorous as that of the rabbi.

 RELIGIOUS BUILDINGS. Jewish worship buildings are called *synagogues*, a term derived from the Greek word for "assembling." It must be emphasized that a synagogue is not the same thing as the temple we read about in the Bible. The temple was a site for sacrifices, whereas a synagogue is a place for prayer and teaching. Still, Reform congregations refer to their synagogues as "temples," partially to close the book on the idea of a return to the biblical temple.

Certain elements are found in every synagogue. At the front of the room there is a platform, called the *bema*, on which the rabbi and cantor lead the service. There is a menorah (seven-branched candlestick) to the side and an "eternal light" above the bema. At the center is a cabinet, called an *ark*, that contains one or more Torah scrolls.

HOME PRACTICES. The home plays a central role in Jewish life. This is particularly emphasized by the fact that some of the Jewish special days are intentionally family-oriented. Even though the Sabbath includes a worship service in the synagogue, since all forms of work are prohibited, a family will spend a lot of time together on that day. Specifically, the Sabbath begins in the home when the woman of the house, having lit the Sabbath candles (the last lighting of a fire for twenty-four hours), says a prayer on behalf of the family.

The coming of age of a boy *(bar mitzvah)*, and in Reform circles of a girl as well *(bat mitzvah)*, is an important event involving the entire family. On the other end of life, the death of a person brings the extended family together with specific obligations to assist the bereaved family. The deceased will be remembered at regular intervals with a special prayer (the mourner's Kaddish), which is repeated at the anniversary of the death (the Yahrzeit).

The Torah commands Jews to remember God as they enter and leave a home, and so they place a stylized reminder on their doorposts. This is a small (about three- or four-inch-long) cylinder containing a parchment, called the *mezuzah*, on which the reminder that God is one is inscribed. Whenever Jews pass the mezuzah, they greet it by touching it with their fingers and then kissing the fingers.

CLOTHING. Orthodox Jewish men usually wear a skull-cap, the *yarmulke*. They also wear a garment under their shirt, from which fringes stick out over the top of their pants. They do not cut the sides of their hair, so that long side locks droop down in front of their ears.

DIET. The Jewish diet is referred to as *kosher*, and it is an amplification of the biblical dietary ordinances. The ancient rules specify that Jews may eat virtually all vegetables. When it comes to meat, four-footed animals must have hoofs and ruminant digestions (such as cows), seafood must have scales and fins, and only a few birds (such as chickens and ducks) are permitted. When animals are slaughtered, they must be drained of all their blood immediately. The Jewish diet requires that meat and milk products may never be consumed together at one meal and that even the dishes used for these two categories be washed and stored separately. Nowadays supermarkets sell many products identified as kosher with various marks, such as a U or a K in a circle. Look for these tags also on items such as paper plates and napkins.

CALENDAR. Judaism maintains a lunar calendar, adjusted on a complicated cycle to stay in step with the solar year, so that the holidays tend to fall into the same range of the Gregorian calendar every year. The Jewish year is counted from what Jews traditionally consider the time of creation, so that, for example, A.D. 2000 was the Jewish year 5761.

The Jewish year begins during September or October with Rosh Hashanah, when the ram's horn *(shofar)* is blown as a reminder of God's creation and the people cast bread on local bodies of water in order to petition God for blessings. Ten days later is Yom Kippur, the day of atonement, a day of fasting and repentance. Right afterward comes the weeklong observance of Sukkoth, the feast of booths, which commemorates Israel's wanderings in the wilderness. This succession of holidays concludes with Simchat Torah, a celebration of the Law.

The next major holiday occurs in December. This is Hanukkah, an eight-day celebration that commemorates how God delivered the Jews from oppression in the second century B.C. and how he provided oil miraculously to keep the menorah lit for eight days on one day's supply.

In March, Jews celebrate Purim as a remembrance of Queen Esther and how she saved them from persecution under the Persians.

The last main celebration is Passover, the remembrance of how God rescued the Israelites from Egypt under Moses. Passover also lasts eight days. It is marked by the removal of all forms of leaven from the house and by a long ceremonial meal that usually brings extended families together.

Judaism is the religion of a people who have made great contributions to the world but who have suffered much persecution at the hands of those for whom they made the contributions.

11

New Religions

This chapter varies from the others in its format. Its scope covers many different faiths, and we will be able to give only scanty information on each of its subjects. For greater details, please consult Irving Hexham's *Pocket Dictionary of New Religious Movements* or Ronald Enroth's *A Guide to New Religious Movements*, both published by InterVarsity Press.

INTRODUCTION. All religions are constantly changing. They have to. Cultures change, people change, societies change and religions are bound to change right along with them. But here's the catch: religions generally abhor change. From the perspective of an established religion, change is usually a negative thing. Whereas in other areas of culture, it is normal to speak of change as progress, in religion it is more likely to think of change as a violation of the sacred order. Consequently, when a new religion shows up, it is most likely going to receive a negative reception and must stand the test of time in order to find itself respected.

DEFINITION. What exactly is a "new religion"? This question is not easy to answer. In fact, the list of such religions below cannot help but be arbitrary. Since it is already difficult to give an authoritative definition for what a religion is, it is exponentially harder to sort out new religions. What scientists call "limiting cases" may help us get started toward an understanding.

Let us agree that Judaism is not a new religion because it is not new. Also, if I decide today to tell people that they will go to heaven only if they send me large sums of money, this would also not be a new religion because it is not really a religion, just a delusion or a cheap attempt to defraud people. Thus, in order to qualify as a new religion, something has to be both new and have the character of religion.

Both of these terms—*new* and *religious*—are ambiguous. Some so-called *new* religions are more than a hundred years old. Meanwhile, some of these so-called *religions* actually have a minimal spiritual or transcendent component. So let's just make things easy on ourselves and say that a "new religion" is a religion that is still working to be recognized, with its own identity, as a separate religion. Still, in order to get a more accurate picture, we should mention that the "new religions" tend to share certain superficial traits. They usually have a single person as a strong leader, focus on relatively simple doctrines and hold out enticing promises to potential followers.

A further ambiguity arises in the relationship between a new religion and its parent religion. Of course, some of them do not even have a clearly identifiable parent religion, but none of them thinks of itself as just another wrinkle on an already existing, valid religion; all of them see themselves as better, truer or more effective than their predecessors. So we must be careful to recognize that the origin an outsider may ascribe to a new religion may not be accepted by its adherents; they may see their beliefs as freshly revealed truths. In what follows, we will indicate a context for origin where appropriate. This list will also include some movements that have been denounced as cults but that are actually legitimate subgroups of established religions.

ALEPH (formerly Aum Shinri Kyo). A small Japanese group (literally, the Sect of Supreme Truth) that formed itself under Chizuo Matsumoto (Shoko Asahara) in 1995 and changed its name to Aleph in 2000. Membership estimates range from fifteen hundred to two thousand. Its religious emphasis is on finding mystical knowledge through Hindu meditation and yoga, focusing on the god Shiva. Aleph also believes that the world is soon coming to an end, and its original teaching included the idea that true believers were obligated to hasten the world's end by causing catastrophes. In 1995 this group carried out a deadly nerve gas attack on the Tokyo subway.

AHMADIYYA ISLAM. An Islamic movement originating in Pakistan. This group is strenuously pacifistic, opposing all use of violence, even on the level of personal defense, let alone as a military jihad. Its founder, Mirza Ghulam Ahmad (1839–1908), claimed to be the Islamic Mahdi, the second coming of Christ and even the fulfillment of Hindu expectations of the coming of Krishna. His followers today are divided into those who see him as a prophet and thus on a par with Muhammad (the Qadiyan group) and those who say that he was only a great reformer (the Lahore group). The Qadiyan group is excluded by other Muslims, whereas the Lahore division is considered a legitimate Islamic sect. The Ahmadiyya movement is important because it is highly active in recruiting new members for Islam and in distributing information widely through publications and the Internet. Ahmadiyya Muslims claim as many as 200 million followers.

CAO DAI. A religion that originated in Vietnam in the 1920s and that has had some influence in Southeast Asia, claiming up to four million practitioners. It is an attempt to combine everything that is best in the world's religions into one homogeneous spiritual practice, including ideas derived from Christianity, Buddhism and Hinduism. Despite its lofty ambitions, the result has become more of a practice of the mystical and occult sides that are tangential to the parent religions.

CHRISTIAN SCIENCE. The most prominent member of a number of groups arising in nineteenth-century America seeking to combine some traditional Christian concepts with the newly arrived insights of Eastern philosophy and with discoveries in psychosomatic healing. In 1875 the founder, Mary Baker Eddy, argued in her central book, *Science and Health with Key to the Scriptures*, that human illnesses are caused by the illusion that the material world is real and that the way to overcome the suffering is to overcome the illusion. Thus Christian Science forbids the use of modern medicine. Its headquarters are located in Boston, Massachusetts.

FALUN GONG (or Falun Dafa). A recent Chinese movement that consists of some simple exercises and meditation in order to promote physical health and material well-being among its practitioners. Its founder, Li Hongzhi, uses some relatively unsophisticated Buddhist and Daoist concepts in order to rationalize the efficacy of his techniques, but it is the practice, not the doctrine, that has attracted followers. Around the turn of the millennium, Falun Gong claimed a hundred million followers in the People's Republic of China, a nation in which any popular movement, no matter how nonpolitical its stated aims may be, is considered to be a threat to the government. Consequently, Falun Gong has been persecuted, and in turn that persecution has precipitated a worldwide protest on behalf of human rights.

ISKCON (Hare Krishna). When the International Society of Krishna Consciousness first became known in the West, it was reckoned among the newly created cults, but it is actually a longstanding movement within Hinduism. Its current membership hovers around one million. As a religious order, it goes back to the sixteenth century, when a man named Caitanya taught devotion to Krishna, but its beliefs and practices are rooted in the two-thousand-year-old Bhagavad Gita. Its most important doctrine is that Krishna is the supreme personal godhead; its practice is the chanting of "Hare Krishna." It first came to the United States in 1969 under the leadership of A. C. Bhaktivedanta Prabhupada, who had just turned seventy years old.

JEHOVAH'S WITNESSES. Originating as a Christian Bible-prophecy movement in America, this group has increasingly distanced itself from classical Christian teachings. Most notably it denies the deity of Christ and life after death for all but a few devoted people. Founded in the nineteenth century by Charles Taze Russell and now headquartered in New York, Jehovah's Witnesses see themselves as constituting a separate nation and do not pay allegiance to the country in which they live, let alone go to war for it. Basing their stand on a literal interpretation of the Old Testament's teaching that the souls of persons lie in their blood, Jehovah's Witnesses consistently refuse to take blood transfusions, even if one would mean the saving of a child's life.

Both Jehovah's Witnesses and Mormons (see below) have been around for a long time, but they still fall under the heading of "new" religions because of their ambivalent relationship to their parent religion, Christianity. The problem is that, objectively studied, their doctrines and those of classical Christianity are incompatible. Regardless of whether they are true or false, neither Jehovah's Witnesses nor Mormonism can be true at the same time as classical Christianity, and yet they seek to be recognized as true forms of Christianity, not as separate religions. Given this deadlock, it is easy to see that, since traditional Christians are not likely to concede their case, both of these groups will continue to be viewed as offshoots of Christianity rather than either as legitimate forms of Christianity or as separate religions.

JUCE. Is it possible that there is a religion with roughly twenty million adherents (more than Jews and Jains combined) that is virtually unknown in most of the world? It is, with a little political sleight of hand. Juce (which means "self-reliance") is the official religion of North Korea and is a lightly spiritualized version of Marxism. All people of North Korea are automatically considered to be members of Juce, and unsurprisingly, the population of North Korea comes out to around twenty million.

MORMONISM. The Church of Jesus Christ of Latter-day Saints began in 1830 in America under the leadership of Joseph Smith, who claimed to have received new revelations in the form of tablets by way of the angel Moroni. The angel told Smith that none of the churches existing at the time were true to Christ and that he was to reestablish the true teachings of Jesus. The tablets, which were published as the Book of Mormon, tell the story of how Jesus came to America after the Resurrection and taught his gospel to the tribes there at that time. Mormonism's distinctive teachings include the idea that human beings can eventually become gods and rule over their own planets. There are approximately eleven million Mormons today, with Salt Lake City, Utah, as the central location. (See also the comment that includes Mormonism under "Jehovah's Witnesses.")

NATION OF ISLAM. This is the American Black Muslim movement. It began in the 1930s completely out of sync with mainline Islam by claiming that its founders, W. D. Fard and Elijah Muhammad (Poole), were the incarnations of Allah and the prophet Muhammad, respectively. The core of their teaching was that the black race alone constitutes true human beings and that other races are evil imitations. Largely due to the influence of the late Malcolm X, in the 1970s the movement dropped its unique teachings and aligned itself with worldwide Islam. However, the more eccentric teachings have been perpetuated by a splinter movement under the leadership of Louis Farrakhan, numbering around twenty thousand adherents.

RASTAFARIANISM. A colorful religious movement originating in the 1930s with the coronation of the Ethiopian emperor Haile Selassie, whose family name was Ras Tafari. In faraway Jamaica some preachers—inspired by Marcus Garvey's philosophy of black self-determination—saw this event as a

sign of the impending liberation of African people and
believed that Haile Selassie was an incarnation of God (Jah).
The 600,000 or so Rastafarians are well known for their dread-
lock hairstyles and reggae music. A part of their religious practice includes the sacramental smoking of marijuana *(ganja)*.

SCIENTOLOGY. Although Scientology resembles Eastern
thought (such as Tibetan Buddhism) in certain ways, it did not
arise out of any parent religion but rather was developed by
L. Ron Hubbard, an American author of science fiction novels.
As stated on the religion's website, its aim is to bring about
"increased awareness and spiritual freedom for the individual
and rehabilitation of his basic decency, power and ability." It
does so by isolating the factors within a person's mind that pre-
vent full growth and by teaching techniques that will bring
about spiritual liberation. Scientology is well known for the
book *Dianetics*, in which Hubbard explicated his understanding
of the relationship between the soul and the body. Scientology's own participation figures could add up to as high as eight
million, but an actual membership number is probably closer
to half a million. Its headquarters are in Clearwater, Florida.

SOKA GAKKAI. This Japanese form of Buddhism actively
reaches out to people around the globe, including Europe and
the United States. It began with the Japanese monk Nichiren
(1222–1282), who declared that true Buddhism must be faithful
to the Lotus Sutra. He wrote a salutation to the Lotus Sutra on
a sheet of rice paper. This paper became known as the
gohonzon, and Nichiren taught his followers to recite the words
Namu myo horengekyo ("I salute the teachings of the beautiful
Lotus Sutra") on a regular basis. This salutation, also called the
daimoku, is supposed to contain great spiritual power, with its
benefits ranging from achieving Buddhahood to receiving
health and prosperity. The adherents spend several hours
each day in front of an official reproduction of the gohonzon
reciting the daimoku. Soka Gakkai is a lay movement within the

Nichiren school, which was given its contemporary form by the Japanese educator Tsunesaburo Makiguchi (1871–1944). The membership number can be estimated at 10 million in Japan and 1.5 million outside Japan.

TENRIKYO. Originally an offspring of Shinto, Tenrikyo (the "sect of Tenri") now considers itself to be a religion in its own right, with approximately two million members. It has been misleadingly called the "Christian Science" of Japan because its founder was a female faith healer in the nineteenth century, but the similarities end there. Nakayama Miki claimed that she was possessed by the Japanese god ("kami") known as Oyagami, who gave her the power of healing. She taught that suffering was caused by spiritual dust that accumulates on human souls, which can be wiped away through obedience to Oyagami. Tenrikyo continues to flourish in Japan, where its adherents believe that Nayakama Miki is still alive, though she would be more than two hundred years old by now.

UNIFICATION CHURCH. Because of the name of its founder, Sun Myung Moon, followers of this group, which began in Korea in the 1950s, became popularly known as "Moonies." Moon's teachings were initially kept secret from the world at large, but since the 1980s the church has publi-cized its doctrines, which consist of a complex set of Eastern concepts combined with Christian ideas. At the heart of Unifi-cation doctrine is the idea that the fall of humanity due to Adam and Eve carried with it physical implications and that, even though Christ brought about spiritual redemption, full physical redemption of the human race would have to wait for a second messiah, Sun Myung Moon. Thus a highly visible aspect of the Unification Church was its mass weddings in which thousands of young men and women were joined together as antecedents of the new race over which Moon would preside. The Unification movement initially made its way into public consciousness because of its highly aggressive—and sometimes admittedly deceptive—recruitment techniques. And we can probably credit the Unification Church for spawning the dubious deprogramming interventions that were used in reaction to those tactics. It probably now has approximately three million members.

WAHHABITE ISLAM. This is an orthodox part of Islam that has given rise to extremist forms. It began as an eighteenth-century reform movement carried out by a man named Muhammad Ibn Abd al-Wahhab in what is now Saudi Arabia. Al-Wahhab believed that Islam was being corrupted by various superstitions, including the veneration of saints. His plan was to purge Islam of all that he considered improper, including the use of wine, tobacco and music. If he had been left to himself, no one might have paid him any attention, but he had a strong ally in the powerful Ibn Saud clan, which instituted his measures when they gained political influence. When the kingdom of Saudi Arabia was officially founded in 1932, King Abdul Aziz al Saud implemented and harshly enforced Wahhabite principles.

Due to the financial resources derived from the oil wealth of Saudi Arabia, Wahhabite Islam has become influential around the world—for example, by underwriting Islamic schools. One set of schools was set up with Saudi money in Pakistan for the training of leaders in Afghanistan. Eventually these students, called Taliban, took over Afghanistan, where for a time they not only maintained a rigid Wahhabite state but also supported the terrorist network al-Qaeda.

WICCA. The Western religion of witchcraft. It does not endorse evil, let alone worship Satan, but instead attempts to draw on the spiritual powers in the universe to promote goodness and healing. Wicca recognizes many gods, including the supreme goddess, who is represented by the moon. It teaches that there are many invisible lines of spiritual power crisscrossing the world around us and that it is possible to tap into them for the sake of helping others. Wicca often likes to paint itself as the female alternative to male-dominated established religion. A membership figure of 50,000 is a highly speculative estimate since the practitioners meet in local covens with no unified headquarters.

Anyone can dream up some new idea and call it a "religion." An outside observer often has a difficult time understanding why a particular movement attracts followers. But clearly, even minimal success by a new religion implies that it is meeting some need that some people feel is not being met by another religion.

12

Parsiism
(Zoroastrianism)

NAME. The fundamental name of the religion is Zoroastrianism, in deference to its founder, Zoroaster, who lived in Persia during the sixth century B.C. After most adherents of the religion relocated to India, they became known as Parsis, which means "Persians," and this has become another official name of the religion. At times, the religion has also been referred to as Mazdaism, after Ahura Mazda, their name for God. In the Western hemisphere, the overarching body is the Federation of the Zoroastrian Organizations of North America.

NUMBERS AND DISTRIBUTION. If it weren't for the historical prominence of Zoroastrianism, there would be little reason to include it in a book such as this one. There are presently no more than about 150,000 Parsis in the world. Their major concentration is in the Bombay area of India. There are a few thousand Parsis in Iran, and Parsis have also established themselves in other areas of the world where Indians have migrated. Because of their relative economic success and social significance, they have been able to sustain awareness of their presence, but low birthrates and strict rules against intermarriage and conversion forecast a continuation of declining membership numbers.

SYMBOLS. The symbols of Zoroastrianism go back to ancient Persia, and it is at times difficult to decide whether they are based on the religion itself, a precursor or one of its ancient heretical offshoots. The most common symbol is that of a winged man, called the *fravahar*. There are numerous theories concerning its origin and meaning, including that it represents Ahura Mazda (God), Zoroaster or the spirit of Persian kings. The most likely interpretation is that this symbol stands for the *fravashi*, each individual's primordial soul. The soul is turned to one side, that of God, and he is holding three rings, standing for the Zoroastrian values of good words, good thoughts and good deeds, which will lead him to eternal bliss. Its message is that each person must choose which side—good or evil—to support.

HISTORY. Zoroastrianism is based on the teachings of the prophet Zoroaster. According to ancient Parsi sources, he lived "273 years before Alexander," which places him into the sixth century B.C. He was a member of the priestly families, who officiated at the worship of numerous gods, called *daevas*. When he was about thirty years old, Zoroaster received a revelation that convinced him that the daevas were not true gods but evil spirits. He learned that there was only one true God, called Ahura Mazda (which means "Exalted Lord"). When Zoroaster started to teach this message, he was rejected. However, when he came to the court of a minor king named Hystaspes, he was able to effect a miraculous cure of the king's favorite horse, which convinced the king that Zoroaster's teaching was true. From that point on, Zoroaster began to gather a large number of disciples.

Cyrus, the main king of the newly combined empire of Media and Persia in the time of Zoroaster, was a worshiper of the Babylonian god Marduk. However, Cyrus's successors for the duration of the Persian Empire followed Zoroaster's teachings. The religion went into obscurity after Alexander the Great conquered Persia, but it came to the forefront again more than five hundred years later, when it became the state religion of the second Persian Empire from about A.D. 200 to 600. When the Muslims took over Persia in the seventh century A.D., the religion went into survival mode. A few Zoroastrians remained in Persia, where they became known as Gabars (infidels), while the majority moved to India, where they were called Parsis.

SCRIPTURES. There is a large collection of Zoroastrian scriptures, although much of it is considered to have become lost over the millennia. The most important book is called the Avesta, and parts of it probably go back to the prophet Zoroaster himself. Subsequent to him, Zoroastrians added many other sections to the Avesta, a number of which, though written in the language of hundreds of years after him, still claim to be his own prayers and injunctions. The Avesta contains a detailed account of the life of Zoroaster as well as prayers, liturgy and incantations.

MAJOR BELIEFS. The basic premise of Zoroastrianism is the ongoing struggle between good and evil. God, called Ahura Mazda, is truth and light. He expresses himself through his Holy Spirit and through the six aspects of his personhood called Good Thought, Righteousness, Power, Perfection, Piety and Immortality. But God is opposed by the evil spirit Ahriman, whose essence denies everything God stands for. He represents falsehood, unrighteousness and darkness.

Furthermore, the previous gods of Iran, the daevas, are evil spirits (note the same root as our word *devil*), who try their hardest to sway people over to Ahriman's side. They do so, not only by tempting people to commit immoral actions, but also by trying to get people to defile themselves ritually. More specifi-

cally, if human beings touch a corpse or any human waste
product, including fingernail clippings or hair shavings, they
are considered unclean and subject to the evil influences of the
daevas. So human beings need to do everything they can to stay
ritually and morally pure. In this way they also contribute to the
greater cosmic picture of helping Ahura Mazda triumph over
Ahriman.

SUBGROUPS. The largest line of separation is between
those Zoroastrians who remained in Iran (Gabars) and
those whose ancestors emigrated to India and onward from
there (Parsis). However, aside from the expected differences in
cultures and customs, there are no major issues dividing these
two groups.

WORSHIP PRACTICES. In Zoroastrianism, worship serves
to exalt Ahura Mazda, to strive for personal purity and to
ward off the daevas. The focus is on light, such as the sun or a
fire, because Ahura Mazda is pure light. In the temples, priests
perform rituals that involve maintaining a sacred flame and
sipping a drink prepared from the sacred haoma plant. Por-
tions of the Avesta are chanted during these ceremonies.
Home worship involves prayers before a small home altar.

RELIGIOUS BUILDINGS. Parsi temples are called "fire
temples" because of the sacred fire that is maintained in
them at all times. Their outsides can be relatively plain, with
perhaps only the fravahar (winged man) symbol distinguishing
it, though modern temples can also be architectural gems.
Because Zoroastrianism has been a minority religion, subject
to persecution, for the last fourteen hundred years it has adopted numerous protective measures, including never allowing
non-Zoroastrians to enter their temples. The inside of the
building is divided into two areas—the larger, plain area where
worshipers assemble and the smaller sacred precinct in which

the priests carry on their duties on behalf of the congregation.

HOME PRACTICES. A Parsi home contains a small altar with the implements to burn incense sticks and maintain a small sandalwood fire. Zoroastrians are expected to pray five times a day, each time preceding their devotions with a short ablution ceremony.

An important part of Zoroastrian family life is the coming-of-age ceremony (*navjot*) that every boy and girl goes through, anytime between ages seven and fifteen. The most important part of this rite of passage occurs when the children declare themselves to be Zoroastrians, repudiate the daevas and begin the lifelong practice of wearing the sacred shirt and belt.

Another distinctive aspect of Zoroastrian practice is the disposal of corpses. Since corpses are unclean, traditionally Parsis have felt that it would be improper to defile the soil with them by burial or to pollute the fire by cremation. Their solution has been to allow nature to take its course by placing the dead bodies on elevated, circular platforms ("towers of silence") and allowing vultures to come and dispose of them. In Western countries, where the towers of silence would not be acceptable, Parsis have had to settle for cremation. Even in India the practice is jeopardized by the fact that a plague of unknown origin is decimating the vultures that are expected to fulfill this task.

CLOTHING. Although there may not be any external differentiation, Parsis do wear an undergarment that is distinctive for their faith. At the navjot, the coming-of-age ceremony, the young person receives a sacred shirt, called a *sudra*, along with a sacred belt, called the *kusti* belt. The shirt is made of white cotton and contains a pocket in front intended to collect a person's lifelong good deeds. The belt is made of white woolen strands and is wrapped around the person's waist three times. At the beginning of each prayer time it is unwrapped and then tied up again.

DIET. Parsis are not subject to rigid dietary requirements.

 CALENDAR. The Zoroastrian calendar is solar. It consists essentially of twelve months of thirty days each, thus keeping the months out of phase with the moon, plus five days to add up to the required 365 for a solar year. Zoroastrians from Iran and from India disagree with each other as to when the new year starts, but they observe the same holidays. On the sixth day of the first month, which falls in either August or March on the Gregorian calendar, they celebrate the birth of Zoroaster.

Zoroastrians take great pride in their religion and their culture, but generally they are not keen on sharing it with outsiders.

13

Shinto

NAME. The popular name for this indigenous Japanese religion is derived from a Chinese term: *shen-dao*, or the "way of the gods." The Japanese equivalent is *kami-no-mihi*, in which *kami* is the term for gods or spirits. The religion consists of a set of rituals and practices that go back to ancient Japan. Unlike, say, Buddhism or Jainism, it is not rooted in some fundamental beliefs about the world, and so it should never be referred to as Shintoism.

NUMBERS AND DISTRIBUTION. Nearly all Japanese people are influenced by Shinto, but few would declare Shinto to be their religion. Just as many Chinese people incorporate various aspects of Daoism, Confucianism and Buddhism into their religious beliefs, so many Japanese combine Shinto and Buddhism in their faith. Thus, if one were to count only those people for whom Shinto is their confessed religion, the number would not be higher than three or four million, but if one were to include everyone who in some way does something derived from Shinto in their lifetime, we would be looking at practically the entire population of Japan, around 100 million. By its nature, Shinto is mostly confined to its Japanese homeland, and it is still considered the state religion by many; it is not something that can be exported to other countries.

SYMBOLS. The most prominent symbol for Shinto is the torii gate, which stands at the entrance to Shinto shrines and marks many other sacred places. It consists of two vertical posts and two horizontal lintels. But let us not forget that the Japanese flag, a red disk centered on a white background, is also a Shinto symbol, because it stands for the rising sun, understood as the sun goddess Amaterasu.

HISTORY. Shinto goes back to a time before recorded history. Presumably it had some antecedents in earlier tribal religions, but by the time we have knowledge of it, it seems to have become a Japanese traditional religion. People involved in a traditional religion do not usually think of their religion as being a separate faith system but rather as being the accepted way of seeing and doing things. This is most likely how it went with Shinto until the sixth century A.D., when various new ways of thinking—Confucianism, Daoism and Buddhism—came to Japan from China and Korea. In response, the Shinto-based cultural establishment started to become conscious of its own identity and to set its myths and rituals into more formal terms. In the eighth century, the emperor ordered one of his officials, Yasumaro, to produce a single coherent version of the Japanese national myth and to write out all the variations as well.

The next centuries saw a tug of war between Shinto and Buddhism for which religion would be dominant in Japan, and it ended in a tie. Because Shinto and Buddhism are so different, each wound up occupying its own niche. On the one hand, from a purely external perspective, there is no question that Buddhism came out ahead. It developed specifically Japanese variations and wound up as the ideological backbone of the samurai. However, Shinto claimed its own ground by legitimizing the emperor and the Japanese state and by furnishing some of the day-to-day spiritual resources that Buddhism does not.

In 1868, when the Japanese government moved drastically toward nationalism and displayed a defiant attitude toward the outside world, Shinto was reinstated as mandatory practice for all Japanese people. The government took possession of and regulated all Shinto shrines, and acknowledgement of the emperor as divine was required of all public officials. Then, when this nationalist ideology broke down at the end of World War II, the emperor was forced to sign a declaration that he was not a god, and Shinto once more reverted to being an all-pervasive, but not dominant, aspect of Japanese religion.

SCRIPTURES. Three major writings reflect the content of Shinto, though we should think of them as descriptive rather than as Shinto rule books.

1. The Kojiki is a comprehensive amalgamation of Shinto mythology, collected by Yasumaro in A.D. 712. Among other things, it tells the story of how the gods (kami) came into being, how a god and a goddess (Izanagi and Izanami) married and created the Japanese islands, how Izanami died and went into the underworld, how the sun goddess (Amaterasu) would not show her face for a time and how Amaterasu became the ancestor of the emperor of Japan.

2. The Nihongi, finalized by Yasumaro in A.D. 725, is a compilation of all the variations in the same story as the Kojiki. When Yasumaro did his research, he realized that not everyone told this story in exactly the same way; these differences are recorded in the Nihongi.

3. The Amatsu Norito is the collection of the most important prayers and rituals of Shinto.

MAJOR BELIEFS. Shinto is not a set of beliefs or a faith intended to lead to salvation; rather, it is a set of practices intended to maintain its practitioners in harmony with the spirit world. Thus the first underpinning belief is that there is a spirit world, and the individual spiritual forces are called *kami*. However, the word *kami* is applicable along a wide range of meaning. A kami can be any of the following: the impersonal spiritual force that is latent in nature; personal spirits that inhabit our environment; or personal gods, such as Amaterasu. The second essential belief is that human beings can relate to the kami; by treating them well, people can harness their power for success in life, while by offending them, they run the risk of the kami thwarting their efforts. As already indicated, Japanese culture tends to leave the weightier matters of the meaning of life and death to Buddhist thought.

SUBGROUPS. It is often helpful to think of Shinto as having different sides. *State Shinto* was the justification of the emperor as divine and the Japanese nation as supreme in the world. This side of Shinto is now officially repudiated, though that fact does not necessarily keep people from believing it. At its peak, state Shinto also subsumed *shrine Shinto*, which includes the holy sites and buildings of the religion. With the demise of state Shinto, shrine Shinto now must fend for itself. *Domestic Shinto* refers to the many practices that are a part of the traditional Shinto home. Finally, *sectarian Shinto* is the term that refers to the many new religions that exist in Japan.

Even though it is hard to think of Shinto, which after all does not really contain any doctrines, as having subgroups, multitudinous groups emerged in the late nineteenth century under the general heading of Shinto, and many more come and go. This is a part of the phenomenon called *new religions* that has now become a characteristic aspect of Japanese culture. There are hundreds of these new religions in Japan. Some of them are related to Shinto, while others are related to Christianity or Buddhism. What they have in common is that they attempt to provide a spiritual shortcut to success in this world by focusing on one particular spiritual being and a simplified set of procedures to make their power work for a human being. Much of the time, the new religion has been founded by a single person, who then presides with unquestioned authority over the group. (See the chapter "New Religions" for two such examples: Soka Gakkai and Tenrikyo.)

WORSHIP PRACTICES. Acts of worship in Shinto are not done for their own sake but in order to ensure personal and national success. Offerings of food or incense are the usual accompaniments to prayers. There is one important duty one must perform for the kami—to inform them of the events and plans of one's life. A kami surprised by events will be unhappy and cause ill fortune to befall the person who did not communicate the matter to the kami.

RELIGIOUS BUILDINGS. Shinto buildings are usually called *shrines*, in contrast to Buddhist *temples*. Many of the larger shrines are really compounds, not just single buildings. There is quite a bit of leeway in the architectural design, but there are some common components. First, the entrance to the compound will be marked by a torii gate. From there, the walkway to the actual shrine will curve to the left (one should never walk directly into the presence of the kami). Along the way, there may be some sacred objects as well as water for purification rituals.

The actual shrine is divided into two parts, the first of which may be partitioned again. The outer part *(haiden)* is the one entered by worshipers. There will be a rope on a bell, which the people will ring in order to call the kami's attention to their presence. Then they can put money in the offering box and submit food offerings, after which they can state their requests or declare their plans to the kami. The inner part *(honden)* is reserved for priests. Here are the *shintai*, the sacred objects associated with the kami of the particular shrine. For example, the shrine at Isé is dedicated to the sun goddess Amaterasu and contains an iron sword, a pearl necklace and a mirror, which are all sacred objects.

Japanese couples get married in Shinto shrines, though funerals are carried out in Buddhist temples. The shrines are also frequently the sites for festivals and the starting points for processions of the *shintai* through the local community.

HOME PRACTICES. Few Japanese homes contain the full complement of religious objects any longer. Ideally, a home should have both a *butsudan*, a shelf or cabinet with a statue of a Buddha, and a *kamidan*, a shelf with prayer objects dedicated to the kami. More likely, nowadays a home will have only a Buddhist item, if anything, and Shinto observances are relegated to the neighborhood Shinto shrine, dedicated to the local tutelary (or guardian) kami.

CLOTHING. Shinto observances per se do not require any special dress. However, insofar as Shinto is the custodian of traditional Japanese culture, Shinto festivals and parades are often the occasion for people to dress in classical Japanese styles.

DIET. Shinto does not include any dietary restrictions. The only kind of food that may not be offered to the kami at a temple is red meat.

CALENDAR. Japan operates on the Gregorian calendar, and all the holidays that at one time may have been scheduled on the lunar calendar now have Gregorian dates. New Year's Day is January 1, a day of purification. February 3 is the beginning of spring. March 3 is Doll Day (also called Girls' Day), when the girls in a family display their doll collections. April 8 marks the birthday of the Buddha as well as the day when the rice kami descend from the mountains. May 5 is Boys' Day, when families decorate their houses with carp-shaped windsocks, one for each son in the family, though some people want to call it Children's Day and recognize children of both sexes. The purification of New Year's Day is renewed on June 30.

In the middle of July there is a time for commemorating the dead. In the fall there are harvest festivals.

Shinto does not present itself as a religion with deep insights into the relationship between life and death, the natural and the supernatural or God and the world. But for those who practice it, its current runs deep in their blood.

14

Sikhism

NAME. The name Sikhism comes from the Punjabi word *Sikh*, which means a "disciple." Thus a Sikh is literally a disciple of his *guru*, the teacher. We're referring not to any disciple of any teacher, but specifically to the disciples who go back to the movement begun by Guru Nanak in the sixteenth century.

NUMBERS AND DISTRIBUTION. There are approximately 23 million Sikhs in the world today. It is an Indian religion, centered primarily in the Punjab area, which straddles India and Pakistan. The Indian state called Punjab is largely governed by Sikhs, though it is not an autonomous region. There may be as many as 250,000 Sikhs in North America today.

SYMBOLS. Sikhism declares its presence with two unique symbols.

The most prevalent symbol is the *khanda*, which represents the Sikh faith to the outside world. At the center is the actual *khanda*, which means "double-edged sword." Together with the circular throwing weapon, the *chakkar*, it stands for the unity of God and his all-pervasive presence. On each side are the two ceremonial swords, *kirpans*, that refer to the spiritual and political dimensions of the Sikh community.

Within the Sikh community—for example, in a Sikh temple—one often sees the second symbol. It refers to the unity of God. The little symbol to the left that looks like the Western numeral 9 is the numeral 1, and the other part means "the only one." So this symbol means that God is the "one and only one"; in Punjabi, "Ekankar."

HISTORY. Sikhism began as an attempt to heal the division between Muslims and Hindus that was causing problems in India during the sixteenth century A.D. Most of India was ruled by the Moguls, who had conquered India and brought Islam with them. Some insightful people attempted to establish harmony between the two religions on the principle that God surpasses human understanding of him as well as the limitations people put on him in the name of religion.

Among these advocates of unity was Guru Nanak (1469–1538), who had a Hindu father and a Muslim mother. When he began to teach, people were attracted by the way he combined Hindu and Muslim dress and observed some obligations of both religions, but in such a way that he always put piety and virtue ahead of formal religious practices. His slogan was "There is no Hindu and there is no Muslim!"

Nanak's followers saw him as more than a human being teaching a message of reconciliation; they recognized him as the embodiment of divine light. They took the ancient word *guru*, which usually just means "teacher," and reinterpreted it as meaning "the light that dispels darkness." When Nanak died, he designated his servant as his successor, and the new community recognized him as guru as well.

Over the next two hundred years, a number of developments took place. The Sikh community grew and eventually established its headquarters in the newly built town of Amritsar. There was increased conflict between the Muslim rulers and the Sikhs, culminating in armed combat. As a result,

Sikhism changed from being a community intended to bring peace and unity to becoming a virtual army, ready to defend itself at a moment's notice.

There were ten gurus during the first two centuries of Sikhism. They all made important contributions, but some of them stand out. The fifth guru, Guru Arjan Dev, collected the hymns and chants written by all the gurus, including himself, as well as the works of some of the writers who had influenced Nanak, and issued this "exalted book," the Granth Sahib, which has been the holy book for Sikhism ever after. Arjan Dev was also the first guru to be martyred for his faith, when the Muslim ruler boiled him in a vat of water.

Arjan Dev's son, Hargobind, began the policy of cultivating a military side to Sikhism when, on his ascension as guru, he picked up two swords, symbolizing spiritual and temporal power. This policy was completed by the tenth guru, Gobind Rai (subsequently known as Gobind Singh), whose father was also martyred. Gobind Singh instituted a military order (the *khalsa*) that any Sikh could join by being baptized with water stirred by a dagger of steel. Male members of the khalsa would all take the surname Singh (which means "lion") and female members would all have the name Kaur (which means "princess"). Members of the khalsa would wear distinctive dress (see below) and learn to excel as soldiers. Gobind Singh also declared that he was the last of the human gurus and that from that point on only the holy book, the Granth, would be the guru for Sikhs. The Granth, like all the human gurus before, was the embodiment of God.

The emergence of Sikhism as a more militant community coincided with the increased presence of British colonialism on the Indian subcontinent. Generally, the Sikhs put their prowess at the service of the British against the Muslim and Hindu majorities that sought to oppress them, although there was also conflict between the Sikh and the British, such as the "Sikh War" of 1846.

The Sikhs' biggest dilemma arose with the partition of the colony into India and Pakistan in 1947. Their area, the Punjab, straddled the two new states, and as both sides were engaged in warfare, the Sikhs were caught between them and suffered horrible losses from both sides. This led to the emergence of several Sikh independence movements, working for the establishment of a new state, Khalistan, and these efforts in turn created underground military activity against the Indian government.

In 1984 a militant minority of Sikhs took over its own Golden Temple in Amritsar. Prime Minister Indira Gandhi sent troops to liberate the temple from these partisans, which they accomplished with much bloodshed. They also exposed large caches of weapons and ammunition. This action cost Gandhi her life, as she was assassinated by her own Sikh bodyguards a few months later. Then, on just about the anniversary of the attack on the Golden Temple, Sikh freedom fighters were held responsible for the bombing of an Air India jetliner. The obvious futility of such actions caused the Sikh community to forgo any further drastic measures, but these acts also resulted in more widespread recognition of the ambivalent position of Sikhism in India and the world.

SCRIPTURES. The holy book of Sikhism is the Granth, which is usually referred to with various titles, such as Guru Granth Sahib, literally the "Teacher, the Exalted Book." It is also often called the Adi Granth, meaning the true Granth. First of all, *granth* literally just means "book," so it needs to be distinguished from other books. But then the collection undertaken by Arjan Dev (the fifth guru) is the only fully authorized version, as opposed to, say, a supplementary compilation made by Gobind Singh, the tenth guru.

When the Sikh community comes together to worship, they chant poems and hymns from the Granth. However, the

Granth's most important significance is not so much in its content as in its presence. As the divine guru, it is the focus of worship and veneration as an object, apart from its message. A typical Sikh temple has a copy of the Granth (the original is in Amritsar), and during the day it is displayed on an altar, where people bow before it. In the evening it is literally laid to rest in a bed, complete with sheets and bed curtains, and in the morning it is awakened and placed on the altar again—both times with special ceremonies.

MAJOR BELIEFS. Guru Nanak sought to find spiritual truth behind the external forms of either Islam or Hinduism. In the process his teachings combined important elements from both religions. From Hinduism he maintained the ideas of reincarnation and karma (the belief that our actions will influence what we will become in our next life). From Islam he took over the belief that God is one and is not to be represented with idols. His message was that by living a life in keeping with divine virtues one would eventually become one with God and escape the cycle of reincarnation.

Nanak was adamant that our thoughts of God should not be limited by what just one religion teaches. God is not just Allah, not just Rama, and so forth, but God is a reality greater than any human words or concepts could encompass. His favorite term for God was Sat Nam, the "True Name," which was not supposed to be just another name for God but was supposed to indicate that God's name is unknown to us and can only be referred to indirectly. By and large, when Sikhs talk about God today, they use the term "one and only one," or "Ekankar" in the Punjabi language.

SUBGROUPS. In one sense, Sikhism has a major subgroup—one to which almost everyone belongs. This is the khalsa, the military order begun by Hargobind, the sixth guru. However, it is not necessary for every Sikh to be a member of the khalsa. Also, even though today presumably the overwhelming majority of Sikhs consider themselves to be a part of the khalsa, few belong to militant organizations.

WORSHIP PRACTICES. Sikhs enjoy coming together for worship because, in addition to the more religious activities, it is a time for the community to enjoy fellowship and affirm itself. The prayer service is simple, consisting primarily of the chanting of passages from the Granth to the accompaniment of various instruments. A leading member of the community (which can be a man or a woman) presides behind the altar, waving away physical and spiritual impurities from the Granth from time to time. At the conclusion of the chanting service, everyone receives a sweet, made of nuts and honey.

But the singing and prayers are just the beginning. Now everyone, including many who did not make it to the chanting service, gathers for a meal. The "common kitchen," or *langar*, may be the most distinctive aspect of Sikh community gatherings. All people, regardless of social or economic standing, sit side by side on the floor, eating the same food together. Even when, during the early days of Sikhism, the Mogul emperor Akbar (whose grandson is known to the world as the builder of the Taj Mahal) came to visit the third guru, Amar Das, he was required to sit together with everyone else. Thus Sikhism continues to extol the equality of all human beings and to repudiate the caste system.

RELIGIOUS BUILDINGS. A Sikh temple, known as a *gurdwara*, is usually a plain building, both inside and out. However, some of the biggest ones, such as the Golden Temple in Amritsar or the Gurdwara Bangla Sahib in Delhi, are enormous and highly adorned structures. More often than not, a gurdwara will have a domed roof, and the Sikh insignia will be prominently displayed on it. The bigger temples have adjoining shallow pools, the water of which (referred to as "nectar") is considered to have purifying value.

Most of the inside of a Sikh temple consists simply of a carpeted floor, reminiscent of a mosque. However, there are two important furnishings: the altar on which the Granth lies during the day under a canopy and the bed for the Granth at night. Non-Sikhs are welcome to visit a gurdwara, but they must wash their hands and feet and cover their heads. If they sit down, they must make sure they cross their legs, so as not to point their feet in the direction of the holy book, and they may never turn their back on it.

Also, of course, in order to host the communal meal, a gurdwara must have a kitchen and dining area. A number of Sikh temples in North America have tables and chairs, but it is hotly disputed whether this arrangement violates the Sikh spirit of egalitarianism expressed by the traditional practice of having everyone sit on the floor together.

HOME PRACTICES. A traditional Sikh family follows established roles, with the husband carrying the leadership and the wife caring for domestic matters. However, such a hierarchy does not necessarily apply to the spiritual life of the family, where the woman may carry a larger burden of responsibility than the man. Devout Sikhs will recite lengthy prayers every day, possibly several times a day. It is common for Sikhs to decorate their homes, their front doors and their cars with pictures of the gurus, particularly Guru Nanak. In keeping with Sikhism's injunction against idolatry, however, these pictures are not objects of veneration.

CLOTHING. When Guru Gobind Singh established the order of the khalsa, a part of its requirements were certain unmistakable items of apparel. They are commonly referred to as the five K's, based on the words for them in the Punjabi language: (1) long, uncut hair and beard, covered with a turban *(kesh);* (2) a wooden comb, inserted into the hair *(kanga);* (3) an iron bracelet *(kara);* (4) shorts *(kachara);* and (5) a sword *(kirpan)*. Even though within their own cultural environments many Sikhs maintain this standard, in the modern world, particularly outside the Punjab region of India, you don't see many people in this garb, except on ceremonial occasions. Nevertheless, the turban is still often a clear sign of someone's being a Sikh.

DIET. Sikhism teaches that physical self-denial encourages a false piety, which may impress others but does not contribute to one's spiritual development. Consequently, it forbids fasting as a spiritual exercise and frowns on any other way of using the deprivation of food in the name of religion. That doesn't mean it encourages gluttony or forbids restricting one's diet for other reasons (such as medical ones), but it does mean that Sikhism does not come with specific food restrictions, such as vegetarianism.

CALENDAR. Sikhs have a lot to celebrate. There are ten human gurus, each with his own birthday, day of becoming a guru and day of death. Plus there is the first installation of the Granth, its recognition as guru and the creation of the khalsa, to mention just a few more. These dates are scattered over the entire year.

Until 1998 Sikhism observed a lunar calendar, beginning with the birth of Guru Nanak in 1469. In 1998, the Sikh year 530, the religion adopted the solar year, thereby ensuring that holidays will always fall on the same date on the Western calendar. But it maintained their starting point and it set the beginning of each year on March 14. Thus, for example, on March 14, 2005, the Sikh year of 537 began.

When you encounter Sikhism, look past the turbans and warlike decorations and think, *Community*.

15

Traditional and
Tribal Religions

An important note: This chapter is different from the others. It does not focus on any one religion. Instead it presents a number of concepts that cut across the boundaries of various religions and are often most at home in traditional cultures. Use this chapter to look up helpful information on

- spirits
- ancestor worship
- ritual
- magic and witchcraft
- fortunetelling
- sacrifice
- rites of passage

NAME. Many people around the world follow religious practices and beliefs that do not have a name or even a clear identity. We call what they are doing a "religion," but for them it is just the way in which one does things. These are the ritual and spiritual practices of traditional and tribal cultures, and they vary greatly, depending on which people one encounters. Ultimately, the only meaningful designation for any of them is in terms of a specific culture. Sometimes it makes sense to talk generally of African traditional religion or Native American religion, but when you come right down to it, you have to be a lot more specific and refer to, say, "the religion of the Navajo tribe" or "the religion of the Maasai."

These religions do, however, embody patterns that are deeply ingrained in the human psyche, and even though the cultures may be far away from modern industrialized life, the same patterns manifest themselves wherever religion is being practiced—and often even where it is not.

NUMBERS AND DISTRIBUTION. According to some estimates, 150 million people around the world are practicing some form of traditional religion in a relatively pure form. Even if this number is accurate, it is rapidly dwindling due to the missionary efforts of other religions as well as the fact that the modern world seems to be simply swallowing up these cultures, religion and all. Still, if we were to expand our criteria to include everyone who has ties to the patterns of traditional religious practice, we would have to include virtually all of humanity.

SYMBOLS. On the level of a traditional culture, symbols are crucial. Symbols are signs that stand for some deeper reality, but often the symbol itself becomes the reality. For example, Native Americans have long admired the morning star and thought of it as representing courage and purity. It is often drawn as a simple four-pointed star. Some American Indian tribes believe that the star itself is a spirit, and others expect that a deserving person who decorates himself with the star will gain courage and purity from it. If you put yourself in the shoes of someone who holds such a view, you may realize how painful it can be to them when other people use their cherished symbols as frivolous decorations.

Nevertheless, symbols are an important part of all our lives.

Even thoroughly nonreligious people wear wedding bands, set up Christmas trees, fly flags at half mast or tie yellow ribbons on trees.

 HISTORY. To speak of history in this context is to raise the all-important question of the origin of religion, and theories on that subject go far beyond the bounds of a pocket guide such as this. It seems clear, however, that to answer this question one has to look at both the remote past—when human beings first started to interact with the spiritual world—and into the human soul to see what it is that drives people to find a realm of existence outside their material world.

 SCRIPTURES. Traditional religions do not have scriptures in the way that the larger world religions do. However, that does not mean traditional cultures do not have any writing, nor that special pieces of writing never play a role in a traditional religion. Often, when something has been expressed as a picture or a symbol, it takes on greater power, just as today in Western society a person may be held more accountable for what she has written down with her signature than for what she merely said. Nevertheless, it is a hallmark of a traditional culture that all important information is conveyed orally, often through laborious memorization, rather than in writing.

MAJOR BELIEFS. We usually associate traditional religions with the worship of various spirits, and this is accurate. The number and type of the spirits, however, vary greatly from culture to culture. Many people believe that there are numerous spirits in aspects of nature, such as animals, trees, plants, rocks or rivers. These spirits want to be treated with respect and not be wantonly destroyed.

Furthermore, many traditional cultures practice ancestor veneration. Here, though, the word *ancestor* is something of a misnomer since a person need not have left progeny in order to qualify for this status. What is usually more important is that, when the person has died, the proper rituals were performed so that the deceased will not come back to haunt the living community.

The important thing to remember about spirits as they are recognized in traditional religions is that they are limited in their powers. They do not know everything, and so they need to be kept informed. They have limited strength. And they need to receive regular offerings in order to be kept disposed favorably toward the living.

Almost all traditional cultures also believe in a Creator. In contrast to the spirits, he (or she) is usually thought of as all powerful and all knowing. The Creator does not, however, usually receive regular attention from the people. In most cases, the people think he is remote and uninvolved, and they usually only pray to him in times of distress.

Whatever the conception of God and spirits, the way in which people deal with the supernatural in traditional religions is on the basis of ritual. This means that they perform the same actions again and again in order to bring about a desired end. Think of the way in which an airline pilot prepares for takeoff. Even though he has gone through the same actions thousands of times before, he follows the identical protocol each time, in order to make sure that all equipment is working safely. If he leaves out a step, there could be serious negative consequences. In the same way, when a culture uses a certain ritual, this ritual must be performed with precision and accuracy lest something untoward happen.

Often a traditional culture will recognize the value of magic. Think of magic as accelerated ritual. A person will have such a strong command of the correct actions that he will inevitably influence the spiritual world to carry out his wishes. Sometimes it is just a matter of a person being extremely proficient at spiritual techniques, but sometimes the person will actually allow himself or herself to be possessed by the spirits, who will then speak and act through the human being. In that case, the person is considered to be a *shaman*.

Magic can also be a negative thing. More often than not, negative magic is referred to as *witchcraft*. (There is, however, no standard terminology, and it's important to note that some contemporary practitioners of witchcraft claim that they promote good, not evil.) In many African cultures, the people believe that whenever someone dies it is because a witch has placed a curse on him or her. Sure, a man may die because he fell out of a tree, or a woman may die because of a disease, but they wouldn't have had that misfortune to begin with if it hadn't been for the witch's curse.

Finally, being in tune with the spirit world may help a person discover hidden connections, which may even disclose truths about the future. Fortunetelling (*divination*) is an important aspect of many traditional religions. Basically, the intent is to establish a technique by which the spirits can manifest themselves with a minimum of human interference. For example, among the Yoruba of West Africa, predictions of the future are made when the diviner passes palm nuts from hand to hand and makes marks in the sand on a tray, depending on how many nuts are left in his hand each time. In the process, he creates a pattern on the tray, which he then interprets with analogies from ancient fables. Yoruba people may make important life decisions based on the outcome.

Once again, even though not many contemporary Western people would subscribe to these practices explicitly, we can see how they show up in less formal ways again and again. We may not believe that the world is inhabited by a host of spirits, but many people do think that their departed loved ones are still with them and watching over them. We may scoff at rituals and hope that we never fall into silly superstitions—knock on wood! We wouldn't dream of having our tea leaves read by Madam Pakvora, licensed palm reader, but we can't help but anticipate how certain things may turn out by looking for little signs. Finally, we might think the idea of someone dying from a curse is ridiculous, but we make sure that we express our wishes for a quick recovery to someone who is seriously ill, and we would be offended if others did not do the same for us.

SUBGROUPS. Obviously, given the fact that traditional religions are completely bound to local situations, it is impossible to think of their having subgroups. However, speaking of subgroups, this section gives a chance to talk about *totems*, a concept that is as well known as it is often misunderstood.

We all know the colorful totem poles that we associate with Native Americans. Not every American Indian tribe uses totem poles; they are most popular among the northwestern tribes, such as the Tlingit. Totem poles usually tell stories, and the most common story they tell is how a person is descended from mythical ancestors, usually in the animal realm. Being "low man on the totem pole" is actually not a bad thing to be; this spot is frequently reserved for an exalted person or a mythical being.

All over the world, however, totems also carry the crucial function of dividing tribal groups. If a tribe were to consist of two totemic groups, say, the "wolves" and the "bears," there would usually be some particular food that is taboo for each of the groups, thereby ensuring that in case of a shortage there might still be enough around to feed at least half the tribe. Also, as a rule, people are required to marry someone outside their own totem group, thus avoiding inbreeding.

WORSHIP PRACTICES. Uncountable religious rituals and practices are associated with the many traditional religions. Think of the great variety in how people engage the spiritual dimension, from the North American Indians' sun dance to an African divination ceremony. Many people, including many of the traditional cultures, find it helpful to distinguish between worship, which is an act of submission to the Creator God, and veneration, which encompasses rituals directed toward spirits. (This distinction is much like that found in Roman Catholic Christianity, in which God alone is worshiped but saints are venerated.)

RELIGIOUS BUILDINGS. Given the nature of traditional cultures, one should not expect elaborate religious buildings on a par with churches, mosques or temples. Nevertheless, traditional religions will frequently have a building set aside for ceremonial purposes. A large number of Native American tribes maintain sweat lodges, in which members purify their bodies and their spirits. Among traditional Africans, the healer may have a special hut, and often the dwelling of the chief is the spiritual center of the kraal (village of huts) as well.

HOME PRACTICES. Traditional cultures do not usually have a distinct dividing line between what is public and what is private, and even though there usually is personal space and personal property, any individualistic attitude that might seek to make religion a purely private matter is unheard of. Depending on the culture, there are specific roles and obligations carried out in each household and family grouping. There is, however, no getting around the fact that what happens in the home will affect the community as a whole and vice versa. Thus a family's not being diligent in their prayers might bring calamity on an entire village. Or, on a more positive note, if every household keeps the ways of the spirits properly, the community will prosper.

CLOTHING. Because of the great variety represented among traditional cultures, it is impossible to discuss clothing in general. However, this may be a good point at which to address the ticklish issue of ornamentation.

The important thing to remember is that what may look to us like nothing more than a pretty piece of jewelry or body art may be of great significance to the wearer. Decorations may indicate a person's standing in his or her community or carry spiritual power. For example, in many cultures people wear bracelets to ward off evil spirits, but if the bracelets are not put on properly or not worn in the right way, they might backfire and attract evil spirits. An outsider cavalierly sporting the "neat-looking" beads may cause consternation among people of the culture. And remember, just because somebody is selling something does not mean it is legitimate or appropriate in the eyes of the culture for you to wear it.

DIET. Again, the great diversity of traditional cultures keeps us from being able to make useful general remarks. But once again, we can call attention to certain interesting features that appear in many traditional religions. For one thing, there is the notion of *taboo*, which is often associated with eating certain foods. There is an important difference between a certain food's just being forbidden and its actually being taboo.

To make up a silly example, if my neighbor has a chicken and I steal it, cook it and eat it, I have done something wrong, but it's my fault, not the chicken's. But let us say that eating chicken is considered taboo in my culture. Then it doesn't matter whether the chicken belonged to me, whether I meant to eat it or whether I even knew I was eating chicken—just the ingestion of chicken would be the violation of a taboo, and I would be ritually defiled and liable to suffer serious negative consequences.

On the other hand, it is also important to remember that in many cultures food is considered a sacred gift from the Creator or the spirits. The Algonquin tribes of North America go to an extreme with this notion. Anytime someone kills a living being, perhaps accidentally stepping on a worm, the person must give thanks for it to the Great Spirit (Manitou) and eat it.

CALENDAR. Once more looking for a general principle behind all the possible diversity, we can make this observation: traditional cultures are usually tied closely to the one-year cycle on which their economy is based, and time does not stretch either backward or forward beyond that cycle.

Let me try to explain by making a contrast. Each December 25 Western Christians celebrate the birth of Christ. They commemorate the event by rehearsing and may even reenact it with Nativity plays, but they know the birth of Christ was a unique occurrence that happened roughly two thousand years ago. In many traditional cultures, the important event is thought to recur every year at the time of its celebration. For example, the Hopi of the American Southwest celebrate the coming of the Kachina spirits from the mountains to their bean fields each year at planting time. They stay until harvest and then withdraw again, only to return next year. This cycle plays itself out over and over again on an annual basis.

There is no beginning or end to time, nor are there truly unique historical events. Rather, when the cycle has been completed, it just starts over. And of course we realize that, even though in our modern world we think of time as always moving on, with the past behind us and an unknown future before us, we still find great comfort in the rhythm of the events that return every year.

Fewer and fewer people practice traditional religions, but their many components continue to be a part of our lives.